The Anglican Church Today:

Evangelicals on the Move

SERIES FOREWORD

by The Archbishop of Canterbury

Outside the Chapel at Lambeth Palace hang two commemorative tablets. One is an exhortation to remember Archbishop Longley under whose Primacy the first Lambeth Conference was held in 1867. The other is a relief depicting the consecration of Archbishop Matthew Parker 300 years before. It shows the various robes of those who took part – some are in copes, some are wearing gowns, others are in surplices. This diversity of dress signals the mixture of modes of faith and practice behind the Elizabethan Settlement.

This is the enduring legacy of the Anglican Church. Ours is a form of Christianity with a permanent tension between competing opinions. Indeed, it is precisely in living with that tension that our tradition finds its particular genius and its distinctive contribution to the Catholic Church.

But if this claim is to be valid, we must maintain a comprehensiveness that amounts to more than mere coexistence. Today the Anglican Communion is faced with difficulties and controversies which threaten to divide us. If we are to handle such issues with honesty and harmony we need to understand the different strands within Anglicanism, and to cherish the subtle but genuine cohesion that it offers.

These are matters for every Anglican to consider as we make ready for the next Lambeth Conference in 1988. I believe this Series will be of great assistance in this, and I welcome it warmly.

Lambeth Palace, September 1986   +ROBERT CANTUAR

The Anglican Church Today:

Evangelicals on the Move

MICHAEL SAWARD

MOWBRAY
LONDON & OXFORD

First published 1987
by A. R. Mowbray & Co. Ltd.
Saint Thomas House, Becket Street,
Oxford, OX1 1SJ

Typeset by Dataset, St. Clements, Oxford
Printed in Great Britain by Biddles Ltd., Guildford

British Library Cataloguing in Publication Data

Saward, Michael
The Anglican Church Today: Evangelicals
on the Move. – (Mowbray's Lambeth Series)
1. Church of England – Doctrines – History
2. Evangelicalism – Church of England – History
I. Title 283′.42 BX5125

ISBN 0–264–67106–6

For Jill Dann, Chairman
of the Church of England Evangelical Council,
in gratitude for twenty years' friendship.

Contents

Preface

I am grateful to Richard Holloway, editor of the series of pre-Lambeth books of which this volume forms a part, for the invitation to provide a popular introduction to the Anglican Evangelical movement and for his helpful encouragement and criticism as the project has, all-too-slowly, progressed.

I accepted, not because I believe myself to be the best equipped to do so, but because I have spent a good deal of my life attempting to interpret to others the faith and foibles of that particular group of Christians within the Church of England towards whom I feel the strongest sense of affinity and among whom I have lived – not always admired or admiring – for forty years. I hope the portrait – warts and all – is not unrecognisable.

My debt to them is beyond calculation but in the preparation of this book I have valued the advice and help of many, of whom I mention Jill Dann, John Stott, Gavin Reid, Timothy Dudley-Smith, George Hoffman, Philip Crowe, Eddie Shirras, Frank Entwistle, Tom Walker, Colin Buchanan and Pete Broadbent by name. They are not, of course, responsible for the result but each has contributed in some way to it.

To Rick and Moira Fordham I offer my thanks for the loan – and not for the first time – of their house, in which to write at peace. To Pauline Gregory, my secretary, a grateful hug for the mass of typing which she has undertaken in getting this book ready for the publishers. And, lastly, to Jackie for more than thirty years of matrimonial understanding and a great deal of patience.

Michael Saward

1

Introduction: These Evangelicals!

I was standing in the gallery of the assembly hall in Church House, Westminster, with a pretty young reporter who had been sent by the Press Association to cover a large conference which had just begun on the main floor below us. 'Do you mind if I ask you a question?' she said. 'Of course not', I replied, 'it's my job to try and help you'. She looked at me quizzically, then out it came, straight from the shoulder. 'These Evangelicals', she said, 'are they... snake worshippers?'

I was only slightly taken aback. After all, a year or so before, I had been interviewed by a panel of eminent churchmen with a view to my being employed on the Church House staff when one of the assembled worthies, a respected layman who worked in the media, asked me, with the air of someone who thinks he has a clincher to settle matters, 'bearing in mind your past experience, would you find it possible to have any dealings with... harrumph, harrumph... er... agnostics?' I took my life in my hands and told him it was the silliest question I'd ever been asked.

They gave me the job as Radio and Television Officer and within three months I was on the organising committee of the 1968 Lambeth Conference. As far as I know, it was the first time that a clergyman known to be unashamed of being within the Evangelical tradition had been appointed to one of the Church of England's secretariat jobs. Thus it was that I found myself standing in the Church House gallery with the P.A. damsel whose knowledge of things Evangelical was, shall we say, slightly bizarre!

So how do things stand, a generation later? Are there still people, in and out of the Church of England, who hear the word 'Evangelical' and, in the flash taken by their cerebral computer, come up with a stereotyped image that is, to say the least, unfavourable and

1

unattractive? Yes, undoubtedly there are. Perhaps not so many as there were? I'm not sure about that. Certainly the word 'Evangelical', in England, is generally more of a millstone label than an asset and those of us who are, even today, proud to use the word as a self-description are well aware that we need to do a little verbal unpacking for other people's benefit if we are not to turn off the minds of those who hear us so described. If that's true of England, it's even more true of the United States where the title covers a multitude of religious groups, some of which really do approximate to the 'snake worshipper' epithet.

This book, then, is about what it means to be an Evangelical in the Church of England in the late 1980s. It's inevitably one man's view and doesn't purport to be a 'party political tract'. There isn't a single 'line' which all contemporary Anglican Evangelicals 'toe' because, and here is Lesson One, the Evangelical movement in the Church of England is a coalition ranging from an extreme which is absolutely convinced that John Calvin spoke the last word (rather a lot of words in practice!) to those at the opposite end whose only definable stance is to go on mouthing, repetitively, pietistic mantra-like phrases like 'alleluia', 'praise him', and 'amen'.

Ah, you say, this fellow is anti-Calvin and anti-charismatic. Wrong! This fellow is merely defining the geography between the North and South poles. Both exist within the Anglican Evangelical movement in England today and if you want to understand something of its internal tensions you had better start from where things are. Then, just to make life more difficult, a lot of other cross-currents flow across the Evangelical ocean. Launch out on it in your frail bark and you had better have a good map and a reliable compass or you'll find yourself drifting all over the place.

The Anglican Evangelical movement in England, let alone across the Anglican Communion, is, then, a coalition. It is one part, even if a fairly distinctive one, of the vast worldwide coalition of the people, and churches, who call themselves 'Evangelical'. Some of those are, as in America, rock-like Fundamentalist bodies. Others, as in Germany, are traditional *Volkskirche*. The range, in terms of ecclesiological frameworks is enormous. The opinions held vary from radical political left to reactionary political right. Not many things go to make up the solid core which lies at the theological heart of the worldwide Evangelical spectrum. Perhaps the simplest statement comes from John Stott, himself a Church of England Evangelical, whose stature within world Evangelicalism is universally acknowledged. Evangelicals are, he says, 'Bible people' and 'Gospel people'. By that he means that one essential characteristic of all Evangelicals is a deep respect for the Bible as God's word, the supreme authority, in their eyes, if you want to know the truth about what to believe and how to express it. The other essential is that Evangelicals are strongly committed to 'justification by grace through faith'. That is the focal point of their preaching. A man can only be accepted by God, with empty hands, putting his trust for his eternal hope of salvation in the redeeming work of Christ who, on the cross, 'bore our sins'. That experience of trust in a God whose promise is utterly reliable to 'whoever believes' brings an assurance that such believers 'shall not perish but have eternal life'. That isn't the whole of the Gospel but it is the essential Good News for sinners.

There, then, in the very briefest exposition, is the nub of the belief which unites Evangelicals the world over. They treat their Bibles as worthy of the deepest respect and they hold justification (or its absence) as 'the mark of a standing or falling church'. How they use those convictions in biblical study, in theology, in ecclesiology, in ethical and sociological matters, and in eschatology is a matter of frequent and often profound disagreement. Almost every group has its own ethos and 'feel', but, however much they may argue and, far too frequently, malign one another in speech and in print, they all know what they mean when they talk about 'trusting in Christ for salvation' and 'believing the Bible to be the word of God'. Whatever the internal tensions they face (and always have faced) they know these to be less important than the nature of the disagreements which they face (and always have faced) with those whose attitudes to the Bible and justification seem to be substantially different from their own.

It is against that backdrop of a worldwide Evangelical movement, far more diffuse and divided than is the case among Anglican Evangelicals, who are themselves nevertheless a by-no-means homogeneous group, that this book is written. It comes from the pen of someone who feels he 'belongs' in the Evangelical world even if there are many times when he feels ill at ease with some particular facet of the movement. It comes from someone who also feels, just as deeply, that he 'belongs' in the Church of England and the worldwide communion, which finds one of its own points of focus in the Lambeth Conferences. Not surprisingly, he often feels ill at ease with the Anglican tradition also. Such a schizophrenia affects most of us. We are men and women whose Anglican heritage is held with love and respect but not uncritically. We may be Anglican Catholics, Anglican Radicals, Anglican Liberals, Anglican Traditionalists or whatever. Both parts of our Anglican philosophy are precious to us even if others argue that our particular schizophrenia is immature, untenable, lethal, or even terminal.

I, then, am an English, (very English), middle-aged, middle-class, male clergyman who rejoices to be an Anglican and an Evangelical. What follows may, hopefully, give you some idea why.

2

Looking Backwards

One of the weakest features frequently to be found among the Evangelical rank and file is the widespread ignorance of, and lack of interest in, history. This unfortunate *trait* is, of course, by no means confined to Christians, let alone Evangelicals, but its existence among the latter seems to stem from a strange conviction that God is best understood if one focusses on the biblical era, plus a period of about one hundred and fifty years following Luther's nailing up of the Ninety-Five Theses on the church door at Wittenberg. After that, nothing much happened until Wesley and Whitefield appeared on the scene in the 1730s, the missionary movement developed in the nineteenth century, and Billy Graham arrived in London in 1954. The most outrageous example of this infantile ignorance that ever came my way was the occasion in the early 1970s when a young charismatic schoolteacher told me that 'the Holy Spirit wasn't doing anything between the time that John was writing the book of Revelation and the beginning of the charismatic movement in the 1960s'.

Such a view, which, not surprisingly, would appal any thoughtful Evangelical member of the Church of England, finds its origin in a misunderstanding of the Evangelical's concern for the unique character of the biblical revelation. The idea that the content of Holy Scripture is uniquely different from all that followed it is no new thing. All the great historic churches recognised this and the patristic authors had no hesitation in declaring Scripture to be distinctively authoritative in the way that the post-apostolic and later writings were not. What the Fathers would not have done was to imply that some kind of divinely ordained Iron Curtain came down in the year AD 96. Yet that is exactly what many Evangelicals are tempted to do. Study the canonical books as hard as you can but don't bother with what follows – it's all too evidently subordinate and derived, at best, and full of dubious theology, at worst, all of which led inexorably to the rise of the Orthodox churches of the East and the Papacy in the West. Fortunately, a merciful God provided the Reformation which put things back in the right direction in the countries of Western Europe. Unfortunately, he omitted for some inexplicable reason to do the same in the lands of the Eastern half of the Continent which has meant, regrettably, deep religious darkness in those parts. How odd of God . . . !

Now that may be a caricature but isn't an outrageous one. Until the 1960s it would have been a reasonably fair description of the way most Anglican Evangelicals thought. I remember only too well the element of embarrassment which arose at the Keele Congress of 1967 when the Greek Orthodox Archbishop Athenagoras of Thyateira and Great Britain attended as an observer and asked pointedly why the draft Report ignored the existence of Orthodoxy in its section on 'The Church and its Unity'. A twenty-three word paragraph was hastily inserted which made a polite and minimal reference to the Orthodox and they have, by and large, been quietly forgotten for the past two decades. Relations with, and understanding of, the Roman Catholic church have, in contrast, been transformed in the same period.

Some Anglican Evangelical leaders, having recognised the danger of an indifference to the early history of the Church and the quite contrasting way in which the Anglican Reformers of the 16th century pointed positively, and very frequently, to patristic authors as their allies in the fight to restore the Bible to its central place in the shaping of Christian theology, have quite recently begun to grapple with questions of theological development. Some certainly believe that much more thought needs to be given to the sympathetic study of those developments which are consistent with the apostolic teaching. Anglican Evangelicals remain critical of those developments which they believe to be inconsistent with Scripture, such as the Marian doctrines, and the development of a ministerial priesthood involving sacerdotal ideas. Nevertheless, unlike their fellow-Evangelicals in the independent churches and the House Churches, they are careful to stress that they see Holy Scripture as the 'supreme' and not the 'sole' authority governing the Christian Church. By so doing they allow, and increasingly recognise the importance of, a consistent development of biblical ideas down through the centuries. In such a way they quite rightly avoid the danger almost endemic in pietistic movements of 'leapfrogging history' in an idealistic (and unrealistic) desire to create afresh a 'New Testament Church'. This quest, rooted in the Bible and developed throughout history, enables the contemporary Anglican Evangelical to share in a sense of catholicity which is generally absent among non-Anglican Evangelicals. This rediscovery of a sense of God, at work through his Spirit even in the darkest eras of Christian history, has a long way to go before it reaches a full flowering but it is an extremely encouraging feature of the more recent work going on in the movement.

In that sense, then, the beginning of the Evangelical movement should not be sought in the eighteenth century Revival or even in the sixteenth century Reformation. It can quite properly be seen as an expression of an attitude, a way of life, and a doctrinal framework, rooted in biblical (and especially Pauline) teaching. Rising and falling on the tides of Christian history, the Evangelical movement has known its wavecrests and troughs and only rarely, in England, has it been held in popular favour. Nevertheless, despite the biblical grounding of the movement, the word 'Evangelical', as descriptive of a religious grouping, is probably first found in the writings of Sir Thomas More, who was using it in the year 1531.[1] Taking that as my starting point, I propose to look at the intervening years, tracing the ebbs and flows.

1531–1633 The tide comes in

In the sense in which More used the word, perhaps the first English Evangelical was Thomas Bilney. He was burnt at the stake in that same year. A fellow of Trinity Hall in Cambridge, he experienced a classic 'Damascus Road' conversion while reading Erasmus' translation of the New Testament. 'Immediately', he noted, 'I seemed inwardly to feel a marvellous comfort and quiet, so much so that my bruised bones leaped for joy'.[2] He had discovered, as Martin Luther had a few years earlier, the Pauline doctrine of justification by grace through faith.

Bilney, to his dying day, acknowledged the Papal supremacy and the doctrine of transubstantiation. His martyrdom came too soon for him to set about the full-scale theological reorientation which would have elevated him higher in the eyes of later generations. John Foxe, in his Book of Martyrs, was forced to admit that Bilney was not exactly a true blue in terms of Evangelical orthodoxy. However, he was the human agent in Hugh Latimer's conversion and was, in Latimer's words, 'meek and charitable, a simple good soul, not fit for this world'.[3]

The Evangelical succession in the English Church had begun with a martyrdom and continued that way for a quarter of a century. Among the more famous were John Frith, William Tyndale, Hugh Latimer, Nicholas Ridley and Thomas Cranmer. Their stories have been told many times and do not need repeating. A scholar, a Bible-translator, a famous preacher, a Bishop of London, and, most improbably, a quiet, compromising, liturgical genius elevated to the See of Canterbury. But they were not alone. About three hundred others, many entirely obscure, paid the price for their Evangelical faith. Add to that those who fled, and the cost, in terms of one or other of the degrees of persecution, did in Latimer's dying words 'light a candle in England'. John Foxe saw to that and the legacy – good and bad – lasted for centuries.

Few people in the 1980s are disposed any longer to play off one group of incinerated Christians for another lot who were disembowelled. The technical reasons may have been different – heresy versus treason – but there is little point in disputing that two substantially contrasting convictions about doctrine and authority were the essential causes of the horrific purges which three Tudor monarchs unleashed upon those whom they deemed guilty. Anglican Evangelicals in the 1980s honour those who died for their faith and even if they think primarily in terms of their own heroes, they understand the similar feelings shared by the descendants of those whose obedience was to Rome first. Not for us any longer is there the wish – which, alas, remains (or so it seems) in Ulster, to:

> . . . revive old factions
> . . . restore old policies
> or follow an antique drum.[4]

The history of Tudor England is a bloody one but it is also a history of the founding of a self-confident nation-state, a monarchy beginning to grapple with the democratic urges within its borders, the lust for exploration and gold across the newly-opened oceans, and the constant fear of invasion by Continental powers. It is against that back-drop that the religious tensions were played out. What relationships were possible with the Catholic nations? What co-operation could be achieved between the Protestant powers? What kind of religious framework could be sustained at home, without risk to internal security? These were the questions facing Elizabeth as she succeeded to the throne in 1558 and was crowned in 1559.

It has often been suggested by the more Reformed among Anglican Evangelicals that what transpired in the next fifty years was a battle between the compromising monarchists and the 'real' Evangelicals who were the forefathers of later Puritanism. This is a distinctly partial reading of history and by no means all Anglican Evangelicals see themselves as being descendants of the Genevan-inspired returning exiles. A. G. Dickens has pointed out that both Jewel and Grindal rejected the proposal of Knox and others that the Prayer Book should be 'Calvinised' and the Genevan way of ordering society be established as soon as possible in England. While it was evident that in the years after 1540 there had been a 'massive shift' from English Protestantism's earlier Lutheran inspiration towards that emanating from the various Swiss Reformers, this was by no means limited to the solutions proposed by Calvin. English exiles were living in Frankfurt, Strasbourg and Zurich and while they mostly shared Calvin's essential theology they 'shrank from the full rigours of Genevan church government and social organisation'.[5] Many of them were loyal to the memory of Cranmer and were quite happy to continue with a church episcopally led and representing the religious face of a monarchically controlled nation. In Dickens' view, they were 'most of them . . . patriots who preserved Anglicanism'.[6] When the exiles returned, 'a crucial stage in the combat had still to be fought, but neither the Catholic nor the pure Calvinist was a contender deserving to attract heavy wagers'.[7]

In the event, the Elizabethan settlement was inevitably a compromise aimed at securing the safety of the nation. It was a compromise but not an unprincipled one. According to Richard Hooker, writing a generation later, 'our state is according to the pattern of God's own ancient, elect, people; which people was not part of them the commonwealth, and part of them the church of God; but the self-same people, whole and entire, were both under one chief Governor, on whose authority they did all depend'.[8] Norman Sykes has decribed the royal supremacy as being the 'cornerstone' of the English Reformation. As a system, says Sykes, 'it worked well enough so long as there was no sharp difference of religious policy between the sovereign and parliament on the one hand, nor clash of religious allegiance between the sovereign and the church on the other'.[9] Under the Stuarts it collapsed and the Established Church collapsed with it but it was restored and under wiser, more moderate, leadership continues to the present day.

The first assault upon the Elizabethan settlement came from those from the Catholic side who argued that the Church of England had departed from the one, true, Catholic church. John Jewel, Bishop of Salisbury, a man deeply respected for his Evangelical godliness even by his most trenchant opponents, produced the classic Anglican defence in his *Apology*, published in 1562. While admitting that the English Church had departed from the papal supremacy, 'from the primitive church, from the apostles, and from Christ we have not departed'.[10] What Anglicans had left was 'the church as it is now, not as it was in old times past'.[11] They had retained the three Creeds, the threefold order of ministry and the two sacraments of the Gospel, clear evidence that they had 'returned to the apostles and old catholic fathers'.[12] Three years earlier, Jewel had listed three articles which were the basis of the Anglican position. First, that public prayers and sacraments must be in language understood by the common people. Second, that 'every provincial church' had the power to 'establish, change, or abrogate' ecclesiastical rites and ceremonies. Third, that the propitiatory sacrifice in the Mass could not be proved from Scripture.

That Jewel's *Apology* represented the defence of the Church of England against the charge of schism is borne out by the fact that in 1610 Archbishop Bancroft insisted that a copy should be placed in every English parish church. Jewel, however, like many biblically grounded Anglicans then and since, was no uncritical devotee of the religious outworking of the Elizabethan settlement. David Edwards suggests that Jewel came near to resignation 'because he did not regard the 1559 settlement as Protestant enough'.[13] He was far from being alone in this. The Geneva-inspired radicals were highly critical and by the mid-1560s these 'Puritans' were beginning to withdraw from their London parish churches into separatist conventicles. From these beginnings stemmed the various movements which culminated eighty years later in the execution, first of an Archbishop of Canterbury and then of a King.

It would, however, be a serious mistake to fall into the trap of too easily handing over the term 'Puritan' to those who defied authority and separated in the 1560s. As A. G. Dickens argues 'the term has been used in various senses'.[14] Narrowed to refer only to Separatism and Presbyterianism 'it lacks any formidable content until after 1640'.[15] Thus, says Dickens, 'it seems most inaccurate to see in the reign of Elizabeth a conflict between "Anglicanism" and "Puritanism" . . . the vast majority of Elizabethan Englishmen who cared deeply about religion were either Roman Catholics or Anglican Puritans. Until 1600 or later that spirituality within the Anglican Church which could reasonably be described as non-Puritan remained rather exiguous'.[16] Indeed, he continues, 'the retention of bishops in no way impugned the Puritan character of the Elizabethan church' since it was 'through that church that it (Puritanism) won its abiding role in the life and outlook of the nation'.[17]

Two consequences of this remain for contemporary Anglican Evangelicals in the 1980s. First, they remain unconvinced by the widely disseminated propaganda suggesting that the Church of England in Elizabeth's time was a via media between Rome and Geneva, part-Catholic and part-Protestant. Rather, Evangelicals argue, was it a Protestant Church, grounded in Scripture and those patristic writings consistent with Scripture, faithful in its Catholicity to them but certainly not to Rome's mediaeval traditions. So, too, Evangelicals argue, the Church of England was a Church capable of containing.a Puritan movement, seeking further reformation, just so long as it rejected a separatist solution or an overturning of the episcopal government.

The second consequence, held even more strongly, is the outright rejection by Evangelical Anglicans of any suggestion that in some way the Elizabethan Church was in reality, through its Articles and liturgy, only 'a modification of Romanism', in the sense that Newman maintained it in his notorious Tract Ninety.

The tensions existing, then, within the Elizabethan Church were largely tensions within a body which was in the broad sense an Evangelical body. They were the same tensions as exist today (even if on different subjects) between those Anglican Evangelicals who especially like to be called 'Reformed' and those who are the General Synod 'politicals' within the Evangelical movement. Rooted in the same love for Scripture they nevertheless go on debating, and sometimes quite sharply, the questions of 'what is' and 'what should be'. Nevertheless, almost to a man, they are quite unwilling to hear siren-calls to secession. Only some twenty years ago did Dr Martin Lloyd-Jones, then of the Westminster Chapel, urge Anglican Evangelicals to leave their compromised Church and join him in a pure Reformed Church. He got a dusty answer, delivered publicly, by John Stott.

The Puritan debate, then, continued throughout the reign of Elizabeth I and grew sharper with every year until in the 1580s and 1590s it resulted in the publication of Richard Hooker's *Of the Laws of Ecclesiastical Polity*. Hooker, described by Norman Sykes as 'the greatest scholar of the Elizabethan church and one of the greatest ornaments of Anglicanism'[18] laid the foundations of the Anglican ecclesiology in which Scripture, Tradition and Reason all play their part. Unlike many Anglican exegetes in the 1980s, he did not treat them as being equal but, as Sykes puts it 'of course, Scripture was pre-eminent; and where it spoke with an unequivocal voice, and particularly in all things necessary for salvation, its authority was paramount'.[19] Here again the essentially Protestant and biblical nature of the Church of England was maintained without in any way conceding to the more separatist groups' insistence on Scripture's sole authority at every point. With regard to the retention of episcopacy, for example, Scripture gave no decisive answer either way and thus, according to Hooker, the Church of England was wise and entirely justified in following a tradition which was very ancient and in no way contrary to Scripture. David Edwards is surely wrong in describing Hooker's opponents as representing 'the Protestant tradition'.[20] What they represented was only one element of the Puritan tradition, itself only one part of the Protestant tradition, in which Hooker himself stood. His tradition may rightly be described (in a phrase hi-jacked in the 1950s by an eminent Methodist) as 'Protestant Catholicity'. It is the self-same tradition in which many Anglican Evangelicals stand today.

Sadly, the growing distrust between the Puritans, of all shades, and the leaders of the Church of England could not by resolved by the production of great works of theological erudition. Hooker may have provided the Anglicans for years to come with a great bulwark but the more overtly political pressures led to much harsher treatment by the Queen and the eventual branding of the Puritan movement as treason. Her treatment of Edmund Grindal, her second Archbishop of Canterbury, was an act of monumental folly. He, a man of real integrity, sympathetic to Reformed theology but unwilling to accept either the Puritans' desire for root-and-branch change or the Queen's growing wish to crush them, was forced to stand up to her openly, by letter, and refuse to suppress a widespread practice known as 'prophesying' in which a group of clergy sought mutual edification and training by preaching and discussing a sermon or sermons. It was, in short, 'Post-ordination Training'. Grindal was given short shrift. Tactless he may have been but if an Archbishop of Canterbury cannot politely – and he was polite – warn a sovereign against the danger of repressing a perfectly proper exercise of clergy training, then who can? Some months later he was confined as a virtual prisoner at Lambeth, where he went blind and vegetated until his death five years later.

With the advent of his successor, John Whitgift, the die was cast. Although he too was sympathetic to the Calvinist theology, a campaign of restraint was conducted against the Puritans at the Queen's behest. On her death they hoped for better things from her successor, James I, but despite a conference with the King at Hampton Court little was actually done to meet with the Puritans' grievances. The King himself told one of their leaders that he would 'harry them out of this land or else do worse'.[21]

As the seventeenth century developed the leadership of the Church of England moved further and further away from the Evangelical theology of the previous century's Reformation. With the repression of even moderate and scholarly Puritanism, and the rise of a brand of High Churchmanship whose conviction that the 'King can do no wrong' was coupled with an Arminian theology and a decorous and ornate form of worship, seemingly more concerned with solemn and splendid ceremonial than personal, biblically-based, spirituality (however superb the music and however splendid the ecclesiastical architecture which accompanied it), the Evangelicals were more and more forced to the perimeter of the Church and many of them found their spiritual home outside it. It was a tragedy for the Church of England, and when William Laud became Archbishop of Canterbury in 1633 the inevitability of the impending collision and its damaging consequences for Christianity in England was hardly a matter to be left to guesswork. The tide of Evangelicalism in the Church of England was about to go out. It would not return for almost exactly one hundred years.

1633–1735 The tide goes out

This book is about Anglican Evangelicals not about the history of the wider Evangelical movement. Thus it is not a major task of ours to trace the development of Puritanism before, during, or after the Commonwealth. We can however say of the years that saw Cromwell and a Civil War; Charles II and his mistresses; Evelyn and Pepys; a Great Plague and a Great Fire; a relatively bloodless Revolution; the triumphs of a great general, Marlborough, in the face of a powerful and expansionist French monarchy of unparalleled splendour, and the arrival of Dutchmen and Germans as monarchs over a growingly irreligious people, that one thing, dear to the hearts of all Evangelicals, was digging its roots deep down into English society. The one really lasting positive result of the meeting between James I and the Puritan leaders at Hampton Court in 1604 was the translation of the Bible which, variously known as the Authorised Version in Britain and the King James' Bible in the American colonies, became the one piece of required literature in every home which made any pretence of literacy. 'The Bible and the Bible only is' declared William Chillingworth in 1637, 'the religion of Protestants'.[22] His own reading of the Bible led him to some remarkably unorthodox conclusions and imprisonment, following his capture during the Civil War, resulted in his death some seven years later. Chillingworth was, and remains, a figure of little general interest, but his telling phrase stuck in the corporate memory of England and the Authorised Version did indeed, linked with Bunyan's *Pilgrim's Progress* and Foxe's *Book of Martyrs*, become the chief reading matter on which the English Protestants were weaned. Since the word 'Protestant' still meant all who were not Roman Catholics virtually the whole of England absorbed its language and knew its stories.

Meanwhile the cause of biblically-oriented Christianity languished. The Puritan movement collapsed with quite remarkable rapidity following the Caroline Restoration. Without a doubt the English had had more than they could easily stomach of an unimaginative Calvinism and, in any case, most of them were, as in every age, suspicious of idealists and anxious to be left alone to get on with the business of living. The bulk of the country, according to David Edwards, 'seems simply to have waited, relieved that the threat of anarchy was over, willing to accept any settlement to be imposed, provided only that it was not Popery'.[23]

Whatever the rights and wrongs of what happened in 1662 (and it is easy to be wise three centuries later) England was divided by an Act of Uniformity into Conformists and Non-Conformists. Over 1750 ministers, and their families, were ejected from their parishes without compensation. As a result of subsequent legislation most of them were forced, as were their congregations, to the periphery of national life where many drifted into a poverty-stricken, quiet leadership of the remaining faithful. Within two generations many of their descendants had become Unitarians. How had the mighty line of Baxter, Owen, Milton and Bunyan fallen!

Meanwhile, within the Church of England, yet another round of trouble was about to arise. The Act of Uniformity and the revised Prayer Book of 1662 might have sorted out the episcopalian sheep from the presbyterian and independent goats but those who brought the Restoration into being had not calculated on a King of England converting to Roman Catholicism. This James Stuart did, privately in 1669, and publicly, in effect, in 1676 when he ceased to attend Anglican services. When he became King, on the death of Charles II in 1685, and the hopeless Monmouth rebellion lay in bloody ruin at Sedgemoor, James made various inept attempts to curry favour with Roman Catholics and Dissenters but he was heading for disaster and he knew it. His flight to France led to the 'glorious revolution' of 1689 and the arrival of William and Mary from Holland. Fruitless attempts were made to bring Dissenters back into national life but all failed. A tiny but influential group of Anglicans declined to accept the new sovereigns but these 'non-jurors', who included an Archbishop of Canterbury and William Law, the spiritual writer, gradually subsided into insignificance as a political force. The history of England in the next forty years from Tory flowering to Whig supremacy is not one of religious encouragement. 'Practical Christianity' was the cry with the 'Divine Benevolence' as the luke-warm concept intended to inspire good works. Hand in hand went an intellectual rationalism which could just stretch to an absentee Watchmaker who had long since set the Universe ticking over. As Norman Sykes puts it, 'this age was by no means one of the ages of faith' but 'an age of moderation, sobriety and convention'.[24] Such a rationalistic mood 'was impotent to arouse the emotions and effect conversion'.[25] In the world of Hogarth's 'Gin Lane' and 'The Sleeping Congregation' it was time for the Evangelical tide to come in once more. In 1735 the tide turned.

1735–1833 . . . and comes in again

During Lent, in the year 1735, a twenty year old boy from Gloucester, 'shy, retiring, and shabbily dressed',[26] was coming, while a 'servitor' (a poor student) at Pembroke College, Oxford, to a moment in time when 'Jesus Christ first revealed himself to me and gave me the new birth'.[27] His name was George Whitefield. Within fourteen months of his conversion, Whitefield was ordained by Bishop Benson of Gloucester, at the uncanonical age of twenty-one. He had in the previous five years gone through a period of extreme adolescent religious fervour. He tells how he fasted 'twice a week for thirty-six hours together, prayed many times a day, received the Sacrament every Lord's Day, fasting myself almost to death all the forty days of Lent, during which I made it a point of duty never to go less than three times a day to public worship, besides seven times a day to my private prayers'.[28] This ascetic punishment he accepted on his search for truth 'yet I knew no more that I was . . . born a new creature in Christ Jesus, than if I were never born at all'.[29]

His conversion at Oxford changed all that. 'Never again', says Archbishop Marcus Loane, 'did he pursue the vain path of the legalist or the ascetic. The long night of darkness . . . had passed away'.[30]

Within a week of his ordination his first sermon was the subject of complaint that out of a crowded congregation at St Mary de Crypt church in Gloucester 'he had driven fifteen people out of their wits'.[31] It was the first of many objections. Unlike the vast majority of his fellow-clergy, Whitefield preached extempore and the congregations which he addressed certainly did not sleep. He illustrated his sermons with vivid stories and concluded them with passionate calls to receive 'the new birth'. The mould from which much later Evangelical, and Evangelistic, preaching would be fashioned was formed. He drew huge crowds in London while still a Deacon in the year before he left on his first voyage to Georgia. 'The plain truth', according to Bishop J. C. Ryle, one of his many biographers, was 'that a really eloquent extempore preacher, preaching the pure Gospel with most uncommon gifts of voice and manner, was at that time an entire novelty in London'.[32]

In the thirty or so years left to him, Whitefield crossed the Atlantic thirteen times, preaching all over England and the American seaboard colonies. At first his preaching was such a novelty that he was permitted to use many Anglican pulpits but when, after returning in December 1738 from his first American visit he was duly made priest, he found that the English clergy were scandalised at his doctrine of new birth which, in Loane's words, 'did not coincide with their views of Baptismal Grace'.[33] Pulpit after pulpit was closed to him. In Bristol, scene of some of his very earliest triumphs, every Anglican pulpit was forbidden him. At the age of twenty-four he took the drastic step, after much prayer, of preaching on Hannam Mount to the Kingswood colliers. Within four weeks the crowds had grown from two hundred to twenty thousand. It was calculated that his voice, if the wind was in the right direction, could reach thirty thousand people. 'Come quickly', he wrote to his friend John Wesley urging him to take over while he went to Gloucester and South Wales. Wesley hesitated, appalled, for eight days but then took his ecclesiastical life in his hands and came. It was, for him, to be the start of a fifty year ministry with 'the world as my parish'.

The two Wesleys had first met George Whitefield as students at Oxford. John was eleven years older than George and brought up in the strict High Church tradition of his father. So was his younger brother Charles. The story of their conversions, following a short and unhappy experience of ministry in Georgia, is too well known to repeat here. Suffice it to say that the harsh intolerance that both had shown gave way to a new love and warmth. For three years, until 1741, they worked in friendship and harmony with Whitefield until the collision came over their theology. The Wesleys were, and remained, heirs of the High Church Arminian tradition which, in contrast to Calvin's teaching that Christ had died to save only the *elect*, maintained that he had died to save *all*. To Whitefield, John Wesley's attack on the doctrine of election and his preaching of 'perfection' as a real and attainable state in this life was impossible to ignore. The result was an Open Letter from Whitefield and a note in Wesley's *Journal* to the effect that Whitefield had told him, face to face, that 'he and I preached two different Gospels'[34] and that he 'was resolved publicly to preach against me and my brother, wheresoever he preached'.[35] The split was both theological and personal and, although the latter was quickly healed, the former was the forerunner of the continuing divide between the Anglican Evangelicals and the Methodists. While the Evangelicals remained within the Church of England (as did the Wesley brothers, though not without serious consideration of the need for secession, especially in the 1760s) the Methodists almost inevitably came to a parting of the ways soon after John Wesley's death in 1791. Though the immediate cause was an ecclesiological one (the ordaining of ministers by John Wesley) the Arminian doctrines taught by the Wesleys and some aspects of the eucharistic doctrines enshrined in some of Charles Wesley's hymns were, and remain, matters on which Anglican Evangelicals part company with Methodists. Interestingly, while few Anglican Evangelicals in the 1980s hold to so exclusive a doctrine of election as was taught by their eighteenth century forebears, many Methodists have moved from the 'all may be saved' (hence the need for explicit Evangelistic preaching) of the Wesleys to the 'all are saved' universalism which finds Evangelism an embarrassment. There is, consequently, probably less theological ground held in common between most Anglican Evangelicals and many Methodists in the 1980s than was the case two and a half centuries ago.

At no time during the eighteenth century revival were the Anglican Evangelicals held in much favour or respect by the leaders of the Church of England. Hardly anything seemed more deplorable to these eminent 'Latitudinarians' than 'enthusiasm', which was their frequent synonym for all that the Evangelicals represented. Perhaps the classical statement of this attitude came from Archbishop Manners Sutton who, in consecrating the first Bishop of Calcutta,

T. F. Middleton, in 1814, declared that his chief tasks were 'to put down Enthusiasm and to preach the Gospel'.[36]

Certainly, the handful of Evangelical clergy who lit and passed on the torch in that century were, in some respects, a fairly eccentric lot. Augustus Toplady, known now for his hymn 'Rock of Ages', had a pen soaked in vitriol. William Grimshaw, Vicar of Haworth, was reputed to have announced that the congregation would say Psalm 119, which allowed him time to visit the local ale-houses with a horsewhip and 'encourage' his male parishoners to find their way to the pews before the First Lesson was read. John Berridge, for almost forty years incumbent of the Bedfordshire village of Everton, maintained that what the men of the village needed was 'the Gospel and a barrel of beer'. A bachelor all his days, he told Selina, Countess of Huntingdon, that 'matrimony has quite maimed poor Charles, and might have spoiled John and George if a wise Master had not graciously sent them a brace of ferrets'.[37] What the Wesleys and Whitefield thought of this description of their marriages is not recorded. As for John Newton, while hardly eccentric in character, his first thirty years as sailor, slaver, and near-slave, endowed him with a story which could hardly be equalled for drama in all the annals of the Anglican ministry.

They were a colourful and lively lot, that first batch of Evangelical clergy. All of them born within the space of forty years they worked in parishes far distant from each other. Walker was in Truro, Venn was in Huddersfield, Berridge in Bedfordshire, Grimshaw in the West Riding, Newton in Olney, and later the City of London, Fletcher in Madeley, near Shrewsbury, Toplady in Devon. There were a few others whose names are less well known, like Romaine, who preceded Newton at St Mary, Woolnoth, in London, but two things united all of them, whether, like Whitefield, they travelled thousands of miles or, like Berridge, spent almost forty years in one small village. The first was that, to use Lecky's memorable testimonial, 'they gradually changed the whole spirit of the English Church. They infused into it new fire and a passion of devotion, kindled a spirit of fervent philanthropy, raised the standard of clerical duty and completely altered the whole tone and tendency of the ministers'.[38]

The second conviction which they together shared was succinctly put in a letter from William Grimshaw to Charles Wesley. 'The Church of England' was, said Grimshaw, 'the soundest, purest, and most apostolical well-constituted national Christian Church in the world'.[39] Make whatever allowance you will for possible exaggeration, that kind of language indicates a deep-rooted commitment to the national Church. There was no way, short of ejection, that men of this spirit were going to leave the Church of England and there is a strange irony in the oft-repeated suggestion that was still being made even as late as the 1960s that Anglican Evangelicals were not really true Anglicans at all! This distrust is well exhibited in the delightful, if sad, story of the instructions given to his coachman by Bishop Beilby Porteous of London that, since courtesy demanded he provide his house guest at Fulham Palace, Miss Hannah More, with the means of travelling to see John Venn, Rector of Clapham, the coach was on no account to go beyond the Plough Inn, since it must not be seen to stop outside the gate of so notorious an Evangelical as Venn![40]

The link between the largely unorganised Evangelicals of the first wave (what a contrast between them and the tightly disciplined Wesleyan movement), and those who came later, was a small gathering, centred initially around John Newton, which began in 1783. This, the 'Eclectic Society' was to be the catalyst from which sprang the anti-slavery movement, the Church Missionary Society, and a host of lesser ideas. The notes of these gatherings were published and demonstrate an astonishing range of matters which interested these Evangelical clergy. As Newton, approaching his sixties, fathered this little group, initially of London clergy, he began to hear two names spoken more and more. John Venn, the son of his old friend, Henry, and Charles Simeon, recently appointed to the strategically important church of Holy Trinity, in Cambridge, were both young clergymen and good friends. In the years ahead Venn and Simeon, together with the Eclectic Society, were to become the leaders, inspirers, and organisers of the second wave.

It is difficult to overestimate the importance of that partnership, and its parliamentary colleagues soon to be known as 'the Saints', and by later generations as 'the Clapham Sect'. Most famous of its achievements was the abolition, first of the slave-trade and, later, of slavery itself. Wilberforce, who gave his life to that crusade, is still a household name to this day.

The era into which the Evangelicals were moving was one in which, for over twenty years, the French Revolution and the Napoleonic Wars stood in the forefront of men's thinking. Almost certainly the slavery issue would have been settled far more quickly than it was – almost fifty years from the first shots until abolition – had not men of power and influence been frightened that the social consequences would bring about something as terrible as had happened across the Channel. Even among the Methodists, Jabez Bunting could speak freely of their dislike of two things – 'sin and democracy'.[41]

Nevertheless, as G. M. Trevelyan reminds us, speaking of the rich and aristocratic, 'when those classes saw their privileges and possessions threatened by the Jacobin doctrines from across the Channel, a sharp revulsion from French "atheism and deism" prepared a favourable soil for greater "seriousness" among the gentry. Indifferentism and latitudinarianism in religion now seemed seditious'.[42]

Religious 'seriousness' needed to be coupled with concern for social change and that long and arduous struggle was largely an Evangelical achievement. Whether it was the need for the amelioration of conditions in England or the saving of souls in Africa and India, the Evangelicals were the vanguard. At home this was often a task conducted with great caution and much suspicion of the stirring of the radical underworld, but overseas it was largely a matter of allaying the fears of government officials whose goal was the maintaining of peace for commercial development and exploitation. More and more it became the Clapham Sect who led the movement since by their power and influence they could effect change which was far beyond the reach of ordinary parochial clergy. Thus, by the 1830s, effective leadership had passed into the hands of able, well-connected, aristocratic laymen. Charles Simeon might have, almost single-handedly, created a new generation of young Evangelical clergy through his ministry at Cambridge and, by his buying up of advowsons, secured for them a continuity of parochial opportunity; but what remained beyond his grasp was the effective creation of top level leadership among bishops and senior clergy. Only three men were made bishops – Ryder at Gloucester in 1815, Charles Sumner at Llandaff in 1826 and his brother John at Chester in 1828. In the manner of the times, one even of these appointments was made for the most dubious of reasons. Charles Sumner, related to Wilberforce, married a Swiss girl on a visit to Geneva with the two sons of the Marquis of Conyngham. Rumour had it that he did it to protect one of the young men and thus he incurred the grateful thanks of the Conynghams. Lady Conyngham, being the Prince Regent's current mistress, introduced Sumner to him on his accession to the throne and within six years Sumner was preferred to eight positions of rapidly ascending importance. After one year at Llandaff he went to Winchester at the age of thirty-seven, having moved from virtual obscurity to one of the Church of England's 'top five' positions. 'The total absence of Evangelical shame, regret or even embarrassment' writes Ford K. Brown, 'that one of their clergymen was raised to the bench in such a fashion is perhaps in itself a kind of indication of the strongly practical nature of this reform movement'.[43] In fairness, it should be added, that Sumner seems not to have sought preferment in this blatantly nepotistic manner. It was the way the system worked in those days, though not all were permitted to benefit from it. As Donald Allister says 'Wilberforce was the only one of those who supported Pitt in 1784 who eventually received no sinecure, held no office, had no pension and was not raised to the peerage'.[44]

Historians looking back to the first three decades of the nineteenth century have continued to acknowledge the achievements of the Evangelicals of that generation. 'The deepest and most fervid religion in England during the first three decades' wrote H. P. Liddon, 'was that of the Evangelicals'.[45] Norman Sykes, while regretting the movement's indifference to scholarship (even though some of its leaders were academics) nevertheless acknowledges that 'its services to the Church of England by the revival of personal and individual religion were great'.[46] Charles Smyth is more generous. 'The most signal and, in fact, unique achievement of the Evangelicals is that, although numerically a minority... yet within the incredibly brief space of half a century they converted the Church of England to Foreign Missions, effected the Abolition of the Slave Trade and of Slavery throughout the British Empire, and initiated factory legislation and humanitarian reform, healing the worst scars of the Industrial Revolution. Has any Church in Christendom accomplished so much in so short a time?'[47]

In 1833 slavery was finally abolished. Wilberforce died two days after it completed its passage through the House of Commons and two weeks after Keble's Assize sermon had launched the Oxford Movement. Well might Charles Simeon, who had a little over three years of life to go, write that 'the sun and moon are scarcely more different from each other than Cambridge is from what it was when I was first Minister of Trinity Church: and the same change has taken place in the whole land'.[48] What he wrote was indubitably true but what he did not know was that quietly the tide had turned.

1833–1933 . . . and goes out again

There has always been one particularly naive characteristic marking out the Evangelicals, Anglican or otherwise. They are, to put it in somewhat vulgar terms, 'suckers for a prophet'. And prophets, in the sense of dominant father-figures, have not been lacking in their history. So, with Wilberforce and Simeon dead, who was to be the next in the succession?

He was not long in coming and his name was Anthony Ashley-Cooper, better known as Lord Shaftesbury. He was to be, in Donald Allister's words, 'the driving force in Evangelicalism, for good and bad, for fifty years from the death of Wilberforce'.[49] Allister, himself an Anglican Evangelical clergyman, is more honest than most in acknowledging Shaftesbury's strangeness. He cites the view of Florence Nightingale who was by no means unsympathetic towards Shaftesbury, that 'if he had not devoted himself to reforming lunatic asylums' he would himself 'have been in a lunatic asylum'.[50] Certainly he suffered from acute depression.

Nevertheless, Shaftesbury's moral influence was enormous. In addition to his campaigning for a multitude of causes in the field of social reform (not just lunatic asylums but factory legislation, vagrancy, cabbies, chimney sweeps, flowergirls, female and youthful mineworkers, the cripples, the blind, the 'ragged schools', public sanitation, farm labourers, the opium trade, and the list goes on and on) he was a major figure in six of the major Evangelical societies. Founder of the Church Pastoral-Aid Society, President of the British and Foreign Bible Society, Vice-President of both the Church Missionary Society and the Colonial and Continental Church Society, Chairman of the London Society for Promoting Christianity among the Jews and a leading figure in the Religious Tract Society. He was, says Allister, 'the only real leader of an evangelical party lacking in outstanding or distinguished clergy'.[51]

There was the rub. The Evangelicals were steadily growing in numbers but it could not be said that they were producing clergy of outstanding qualities of leadership. At the one moment in the nineteenth century when Evangelicals just might have taken over the Church of England's leadership (1855–65) they simply could not provide enough men of the calibre required.

Palmerston was Prime Minister. Shaftesbury's wife was, in all probability, his illegitimate daughter. Shaftesbury it was, therefore, whom Palmerston consulted for suitable names to fill the various sees to which it was his rather boring duty to appoint bishops. 'Episcopal bricks', comments Georgina Battiscombe, Shaftesbury's biographer, 'had to be made without straw'.[52] David Edwards wryly remarks that Shaftesbury produced 'nineteen hard-working, if dull, pastors'.[53]

For the Evangelical movement it was a tragedy. Given at last the opportunity to prove themselves not just as godly pastors, heroic missionaries, or social visionaries, they simply hadn't got what it was going to take to hold the Church of England on its historic course in the surging currents which were pulling it this way and that. 'Had there been', adds Georgina Battiscombe, 'even one Evangelical of the calibre of the Broad Churchman Tait or the High Churchman Samuel Wilberforce, son of William, to be appointed Archbishop, or had there been a fair sprinkling of able men to fill lesser sees and to exercise some influence in the Church, the era of the "Shaftesbury bishops" might have marked the opening of a golden age for Evangelicalism. Nothing of the sort occurred; instead Evangelicalism continued to decline, as Shaftesbury himself saw all too clearly. "The Evangelical body, once so powerful, is in fact disappearing" he wrote on April 16th 1865'.[54] Owen Chadwick sums the period up with incisive, if somewhat barbed, clarity when he remarks that 'ten years of Palmerston continued to raise the authority and lower the prestige of the evangelical party'.[55] Such patronage 'lifted them from the pulpit ... where they spoke words of life and buttoned them in a pillory of gaiters'.[56]

So what were the Anglican Evangelical clergy of that era up to? They were doing the usual parochial things which caring pastors and preachers do. They were, to quote Owen Chadwick again, 'steadily raising the ideal expected of the Christian pastor. For many years they had been proclaiming standards which were slowly leavening the popular notion of the Christian minister'.[57] In addition they were pressing, more insistently, the needs of 'the mission field' in Africa and India and, in later years, China. Some of them were, cautiously, involved in the founding of an 'Evangelical Alliance' with Evangelicals outside the Church of England. Others of them were committed to the support of those brash and sentimental Americans, Moody and Sankey, whose missions touched a responsive chord in British hearts.

Evangelical vicarages were, nevertheless, places of considerable anxiety. Two other disturbing influences were threatening much of what they stood for. Since 1833 the followers of Keble and Newman were making their increasingly extreme views more and more widely known. Some of the best known had, fortunately, departed for Rome but the coming generation were beginning to dress like Popish Priests and decorate their churches in fashions long since dead and gone. They were founding monasteries and nunneries and calling each other 'Father' and getting up to the most disreputable, thoroughly un-Anglican, ritual and liturgical practices. Worse still, they were maintaining that it was *they* who stood for historic Anglicanism and that the Reformation was a disaster. To the horror of those pious Evangelicals, the powers-that-be appeared to be capitulating to these influences with indecent haste. Everything–Gothic architecture, romantic music, all the arts, all seemed to have been swept along in a crazy desire to put a mediaeval face (and therefore a pre-Reformation face) on to the good solid classical traditions of Mr John Bull. They, the Evangelicals, were, it seemed, alone in resisting this threat and they would have to look to the Courts to uphold the law.

Bishop Colin Buchanan describes what happened next. The Evangelicals 'duly fought, but with a growing sense of desperation. The Public Worship Regulation Act 1874, far from being the point where discipline was reasserted, became instead the point from which it was clear that the law could not be and would not be forced against Anglo-Catholicism'.[58] The final battle was fought in 1890 when it was required, by the 'Lincoln Judgment', that a priest, celebrating the Holy Communion facing Eastward, should turn towards the congregation for the actual consecration and fraction of the bread. Within a few years all but the committed Evangelicals were taking the 'Eastward position' and, amazingly, assumed that they were obeying the Book of Common Prayer by so doing! Those who remained at the 'North Side', obedient to the tradition of four hundred years were before long regarded as some kind of primeval throw-back.

The consequences of these legal battles were not, however, confined to the place and manner in which eucharistic liturgies were performed. Far more damaging to the Evangelical cause was the bitterness of spirit, on both sides, which lasted for well over half a century afterwards. To the rest of the church, Evangelicals were legalistic, narrow-minded, hard-faced bigots who were prepared to put their brother clergy into prison for trivial liturgical and sartorial reasons. Enormous damage was done and the final vestiges of its impact are still with us in the 1980s.

The second, and even more wide-ranging, threat to the Evangelicals of the 1860s and 1870s was the explosion of liberal ideas. Darwin's *Origin of the Species* presented even Bishop Samuel Wilberforce with the possibility that his forebears might have been monkeys. But it was not just Darwin and evolution. There was *Essays and Reviews* with its denials of biblical inspiration and there was *Ecce Homo* with an attitude towards the atonement which omitted all that was propitiatory. Shaftesbury, in language hardly moderate or calculated to encourage thoughtful debate, called the latter 'the most pestilential book ever vomited from the jaws of Hell'.[59] It might gladden Evangelical hearts to shout insults but it did not help them to get to grips with the new theology or with the scientific revolution that was breaking upon them. 'By the turn of the century', says Buchanan, 'they felt themselves not only surrounded but actually borne down, by the Pharisees, who added ceremonial and formalistic burdens to the word of the Lord, and Sadducees who denied the force and power of it'.[60]

It was all very ironical. According to G. R. Balleine, the historian of the Anglican Evangelical movement, writing half a century later, 'the closing years of the Nineteenth century found the Evangelicals stronger than at any previous period'.[61] Numbers, then, they had. What they had lost was respect. According to Thomas Arnold an Evangelical was 'a good Christian with a low understanding, a bad education, and ignorance of the world'.[62] It was simply no good pointing to numbers as if they alone answered the critics. The Evangelicals had missed their chance. 'Morally,' Donald Allister declares, 'the Victorian era was a triumph for evangelicals. Intellectually and ideologically it was not'.[63]

Between the turn of the century and the year 1916 a rosy liberal glow of optimism diffused much of respectable English society. Man really was at last beginning to be the master of his environment. C. S. Lewis parodied it with the eye of a pathologist dissecting a body. 'Lead us, Evolution, lead us, up the future's endless stair'.[64] Even the beginning of a war between the major European powers could be perceived as 'swimmers into cleanness leaping'.[65] The obscenities of the Somme, Verdun, and Passchendaele brought forth the soldiers' anguished cry 'O Jesus, make it stop'.[66] But, despite Siegfried Sassoon's plea, Jesus did not appear to be acting as Military Policeman and it went on and on till twelve million were dead. The shock to the system, nationally, was devastating. The kind old God who hovered up in the sanctuary during Matins seemed indifferent to all the suffering. The harsh old God who consigned sinners to hell did not seem to have the power to keep the Kaiser and his hordes in detention let alone in hell. It was, of course, the old English desire to have your theological cake and eat it. If you wanted to be free to follow your monkey ancestors who hadn't, after all, been created by God (even supposing there was one) then you couldn't reasonably ask for men to be turned back into acquiescent puppets, obeying the heavenly string-puller when the monkeys got out of hand. Unfortunately the Englishman's theology wasn't sophisticated enough to see that.

The result was a box on the ears for the Church of England. She had lent her support when the Recruiting Sergeants were around in 1914 and she had provided chaplains to go with them (even if

Siegfried Sassoon's had told them that God would go with them into the trenches while he, the chaplain, would go with them to the railway station).[67] Now, for all the English cared, God could go to hell and they, for their part, certainly wouldn't go to church.

Of course, it was hardly ever put so crudely. But the War did hugely undermine the churches and when it was over, instead of mounting an Evangelistic programme aimed at bringing hope in 'The Waste Land', they settled for a decade of Prayer Book reform. They made just the same mistake in 1945 only then it was Canon Law which seemed so vitally important to Archbishop Geoffrey Fisher.

Among the Evangelicals the old battles continued. The only difference was that now they were tearing each other apart. Liberal theology had seeped into their own heartland and even their greatest mission agency, the Church Missionary Society, had leading men who no longer saw the Bible as reliable, or believed in a substitutionary atonement. Just as three years before, in 1919, the Cambridge Inter-Collegiate Christian Union's leaders had turned their backs on the Student Christian Movement when the latter's leaders had declined 'to put the atoning blood of Jesus Christ *central* in its beliefs',[68] so a division on similar grounds took place in the ranks of the C.M.S. As a result, the Bible Churchmen's Missionary Society was founded which in due course created its own theological college, later to be known as Tyndale Hall and, forty years later, one of the elements which went into the formation of Trinity College in Bristol. To the men of the newly formed Inter-Varsity Fellowship (since 1975 known as the Universities' and Colleges' Christian Fellowship) and the Bible Churchmen's Missionary Society, the truth of Evangelical religion, as they understood it, was at stake. Looked back at some sixty years later, it is at least arguable that they were, in essentials, right even if at the time the bitterness generated was to remain throughout the lifetime of many of the participants on both sides.

No sooner was the internal battle settled than the struggle over Prayer Book reform became predominant. In this matter there was no way in which the Evangelicals could hope to persuade the Church Assembly to put a brake on the proposed new book. By a total of 517 votes to 133 the three houses of Bishops, Clergy and Laity gave it their Final Approval on 6th July 1927. This agreement was supported by the House of Lords. When the matter came before the House of Commons and they defeated it by a majority of thirty-three votes the shock waves were colossal. One year later, after certain minor changes had been made, the Book came again before the Commons and was again defeated, this time by a somewhat larger majority.

Randle Manwaring, in his recent history of Anglican Evangelicals since 1914, records that the battle cry of those who favoured the 1928 Book on its return to Parliament was 'Trust the Bishops'.[69] It was an unfortunate plea because the Bishops had for almost fifty years turned a blind eye to repeated illegalities and had, in many instances, declined to carry out the findings of the Royal Commission on Ecclesiastical Discipline of 1904. That Parliament was right to exercise caution in this matter was borne out by the Bishops' reaction to the Book's second defeat in first allowing, and then implementing, Convocation's illegal authorisation of the use of the Book during 'the present emergency'. The 'emergency' was conceived to be in force for over thirty years. Evangelicals, not surprisingly, found it somewhat difficult to 'trust the Bishops' throughout the whole period. Not till the 1960s for many, and till the present day for some, was that trust forthcoming. The Evangelicals of that era may not have been clever men but they were not fools.

What was it that so disturbed Evangelicals about the 1927–28 Prayer Books? There were a number of factors. First the context gave them no grounds for confidence. For some fifty years they had watched the aggressive 'Romanising' process gaining ground in liturgy and ecclesiology. Time after time the Courts had declared many of the innovations to be illegal within the Church of England and a Royal Commission had supported this view. The Commission had specifically singled out certain bishops, who, 'disagreeing with the judgements in some of the well-known ritual suits ... regard themselves as justified ... in allowing the clergy to adopt or continue certain practices which those judgements declared to be illegal'.[70] They add that the growth of the excesses 'was in considerable degree assisted by the inaction of the bishops, especially in the diocese of London'.[71] In such a situation, the alteration of the Book of Common Prayer in order to introduce items deliberately calculated to present a 'Catholic' flavour to the service of Holy Communion, was bound to cause controversy.

Such items included a prayer of oblation within the Consecration Prayer, an epiclesis upon the elements themselves ('bless and sanctify ... these thy gifts'), the introduction of the practice of reserving the sacrament, the use of a chasuble, wafers, and a mixed chalice and the admission of Corpus Christi (with all its associations) to the Calendar. It was not then surprising that, since some of these were illegal within the Church of England, strong and vocal opposition was raised.[72]

So, at the nadir of their fortunes, successful only in having quietly but effectively aroused the innate fear of Popery in enough Members of Parliament to defeat the Church over its new liturgy, what were these Evangelicals like? Randle Manwaring, a young man at the time, recalls their lifestyle. 'They were ... a separated people and their contact with non-Christians was minimal ... their sub-culture was of their own making ... they contributed little or nothing to political life or social well-being ... they regarded the ordained ministry and missionary work as the highest calling ... the Evangelical Anglican was a very moral person, he paid twenty shillings to the pound, was hard working and a sound family man ... he liked sport ... and never went to a pub'.[73] Manwaring adds that, 'between-the-wars Evangelicals inclined to the view that they were excused culture, scholarship and intellectual exercise on religious grounds and they felt exonerated from loving God with their minds. It was all part of their "backs-to-the-wall" attitude'.[74]

This depressing picture is alleviated by one thing only. These Evangelicals remained faithful to those aspects of biblical truth which most touch individual hearts. They offered, says Manwaring, 'a sure foundation for the bewildered, a peace for the disturbed in mind, and, as well as a present salvation, an assurance for the future. They did not change their tune with the times and many sirens did not lure them from their anchorage'.[75]

So it was, then, that in 1933 two events took place, whose German origins were to have immense consequences for their world. The first brought nothing but tragedy and horror through the coming of Adolf Hitler to absolute power. The second brought light and hope and a mortal blow to liberal Christianity. It was the publication, in English, of Karl Barth's *Commentary on the Epistle to the Romans*. Once again it became intellectually possible to speak with confidence of the great, timeless truths for which the Evangelicals stood – sin, grace, justification, forgiveness and resurrection. By any standard 1933 was a year of significance. The tide was running again.

3

Looking Around

Whether it was ever true as Hensley Henson alleged, that the Anglican Evangelicals were 'an army of illiterates, generalled by octogenarians'[76] (their leaders at the time were in their fifties and sixties) it certainly hasn't been so since the Second World War. As all informed commentators know well, the situation of Evangelicals in the Church of England has, in the last thirty-five years, changed out of all recognition.

Why did this happen and what caused it? It may be true that Barth's *Commentary* on Romans was published in English in 1933 and ushered in a new era of biblical thinking but it would be a gross exaggeration to suggest that this one fact was of crucial significance to the Evangelicals of the 1930s and 1940s. Indeed it is more than likely that most of them never read Barth or put much store on the importance of what he had written. Even in the theological colleges of the 1950s, Barth's name was no more than peripheral to many students. So what was it that triggered off the major transformation that took place?

From this point on, this book is bound to become more personal because the era of change and consolidation almost exactly corresponds to my own experience since I became an undergraduate reading Theology in 1952 and in many areas which will be considered the events and personalities have all been known to me. I can hardly apologise for this but it will inevitably colour my own perceptions and may mean that the explanation of what has happened will be better done by historians in fifty years time.

During my early childhood years, in the 1930s, two decisions were made which were to have immense consequences for the post-war generation. Those of us most affected, directly or indirectly, knew nothing about them at the time. Awareness came later.

The first was the decision by a public school chaplain to run a highly elitist summer camp for 'Key boys from Key Schools'.

The chaplain was, in the manner of those days, known by the nickname 'Bash' and his top-drawer camps at Iwerne Minster in Dorset became, inevitably, 'Bash Camps'. E. J. H. Nash (hence 'Bash') was a man of vision. In the 1930s it would have occasioned little hostility to work on the assumption that future leaders in the Church of England would come from the top Public Schools and it was from these that 'Bash' invited his campers. Thus, among others, John Stott (Rugby), Michael Green (Clifton), and Dick Lucas (Radley) came to a committed Christian faith through the ministry of 'Bash' and his camps. Social change, in the event, proved 'Bash' wrong and none of his 'converts' has been given high episcopal office; not least, perhaps, because nowadays only a small number of diocesan bishops are chosen from among those who were educated at the top public schools, and also because 'Bash' discouraged his men from getting involved in Church of England internal politics and, as a result, his most famous trio have largely exercised their hugely influential ministries within the Evangelical world and especially among its more interdenominational areas. However, even if 'Bash' was ultimately frustrated, many men of great ability were ordained to the Anglican ministry whose early years were deeply influenced by his work.

Second, and perhaps even more important, was the creation in 1938 of the Biblical Research Committee under the auspices of the Inter-Varsity Fellowship. Most Evangelical students join the various University Christian Unions but the founders of the B.R.C. saw the need for training a new generation of biblical scholars within the conservative tradition who would have the ability to take up university teaching posts. These would need to acquire the necessary post-graduate degrees and might need help in financing their work. The B.R.C. also set in motion the creation of a new generation of biblical commentaries on the Hebrew and Greek texts together with a high quality one-volume Bible Commentary and Bible Dictionary. The B.R.C. was an inter-denominational body but it was laying new theological foundations which all Evangelicals would be happy to use in the strengthening of their own convictions. Among those deeply involved in its early years was a brilliant young law graduate from Cambridge, J. N. D. Anderson, who, as Sir Norman Anderson, was to be an outstanding Anglican Evangelical lay leader in the 1960s and 1970s and Chairman of the General Synod's House of Laity.

Thus it was that a new generation of upper-class leaders was created for the movement and a new, highly professional, approach to the theological equipping of this new generation was undertaken. Fifteen years later the two acorns had grown into sturdy young oak trees and from them came a new confidence both in the Bible and also in their own ability to expound it, under God, to the building up of his Church.

Randle Manwaring adds a third strand to the other two in his reading of the situation. He cites the Crusaders' Union of Bible Classes which had worked for many years among boys from middle-class homes, most of whom in those days were pupils at the smaller public schools, or those taking day boys, plus the direct grant and grammar schools. Through regular Sunday afternoon Bible Class teaching and summer camps the Crusaders reached young men and boys who, in many cases, rarely went to church. Among those brought to faith in this way John Taylor (Bishop of St Albans) and Keith Sutton (Bishop of Lichfield) are well-known names. I also came to faith through this movement in 1946. Again, many clergy and future lay leaders gained their basic understanding of the faith through Crusaders, though it has to be admitted that a fair number did not remain within the Evangelical tradition, possibly due to the indifference of some Crusader leaders to the strengthening of links with local churches.

Undoubtedly the focal figure of the new movement was John Stott. The son of an eminent London physician, Stott was ordained in 1945 to a curacy at All Souls, Langham Place, in the heart of London's shopping world and next to the British Broadcasting Corporation. Within five years he was appointed Rector, at the age of twenty-nine, and so began a teaching ministry which continues to this day and which has made him a figure of world-wide reputation. The speed with which he achieved pre-eminence among the younger Anglican Evangelicals was remarkable. By 1954 he was clearly accepted by the majority of Evangelical ordinands as the outstanding figure of the future and for thirty years that confidence has not been withdrawn, though his more recent work has probably made him better known across the world than he is to contemporary English clergy in the under thirty-five age group.

In the years 1950–1967 Stott's influence was especially evident in four significant areas. First, All Souls' Church became far and away the best attended parish church in Central London. Its teaching ministry was conducted at a high level of biblical exposition in a convinced but cool manner. No-one could successfully sustain the charge of 'emotionalism' but nevertheless large numbers of younger adults came to faith and the church's ministry developed in many directions. Stott's second area of influence was in the field of university missions conducted under the auspice of the various Christian Unions. He was extremely successful in gaining a hearing for the Christian gospel at Oxford and Cambridge and the Christian Union numbers at both Universities grew to between three and five hundred. In other universities, inspired by his example, numbers grew and at Bristol, which had two Anglican Evangelical theological colleges in the vicinity, the Christian Union grew from thirty to a hundred and fifty in the space of one academic year (1953–54). A third event in which Stott was deeply involved was the first London Crusade of Dr Billy Graham at Harringay Arena in the Spring of 1954. Nothing like this had been seen in London for many years though in the years between 1946 and 1954 many Evangelistic campaigns – the language was always militaristic – had been conducted throughout England, partly at the inspiration of the Church Assembly report 'Towards the Conversion of England' which, sadly, the Church of England effectively shelved in favour of Canon Law revision. Graham's London crusade produced many new ordinands.

As regards the development of Anglican Evangelical clergy, Stott's most important, and strategic, decision was to resurrect, in 1955, the Eclectic Society, long since defunct after its 1783 founding by John Newton. In its new incarnation, membership was restricted to Anglican Evangelical clergy under the age of forty and a limit of forty members was set. Most of its first members were, in fact, 'Bash' men, almost entirely from Oxford and Cambridge, and it was strictly a private, 'by invitation only', society. When in late 1958, it, amoeba-like, divided into two North and South of the Thames societies, membership was highly prized, and withdrawn from any who failed to attend regularly. The Eclectic Society's purpose was, in the words of Peter Williams, sometime editor of *Churchman* magazine, to provide 'a forum in which younger evangelicals could debate and explore outside the boundaries set by their elders. Their fresh understanding', he adds, 'did much to shape the new directions explored further at Keele and Nottingham, and to re-emphasize a determination to make an evangelical contribution fully within, rather than half outside, the Church of England'.

For myself, I can only add that I counted myself fortunate that I was a member of Eclectics for fourteen consecutive years, second only, as far as I know, in terms of continuity of membership to John Stott. Year by year Eclectics grew, spreading out new branches all over England. It was for me, far and away the most important influence on my development as an Anglican Evangelical clergyman, opening up new ideas and strategies which would have been quite impossible to debate or implement within the older 'Diocesan Evangelical Unions', which in those days were dominated by men from the pre-war years and who were, in many cases, deeply suspicious of change. I shall return, later in the book, to the actual influence exercised by the Eclectic Society, especially in the 1960s.

The scene is set then for a brief survey of ten areas in which the Anglican Evangelicals have developed their own particular style (or styles) in the past twenty-five years. During these years the walls of the ghetto tumbled and fell. What came out from behind those walls was a group of men (and, later, of women also) who saw no cause for embarrassment at calling themselves 'Evangelicals' and who believed that the Church of England needed them as they needed it.

Numerical growth

Assessing the numerical growth of any movement in the Church of England can only be done with any confidence at three points, namely, the number of ordinands at the theological colleges which best represent the tradition (whatever it is); the number of working clergy known to be identified with the movement (more uncertain) and, finally, the number appointed as archdeacons, deans, provosts, and bishops. Influence – that indefinable thing – in universities, public life generally, and the mass media is much more difficult to quantify.

In the 1870s, J. C. Ryle – later to become Bishop of Liverpool – calculated that about 20% of the clergy were Evangelicals. By the turn of the century, if G. R. Balleine is right, 'fully a quarter of the parishes in England were in their hands'.[77] By the time that the new Prayer Book was before the Church Assembly (1927) the percentage of clergy voting against its adoption was just under 13%. Since it was, by and large, only Evangelicals who opposed the book, we have some idea of their numbers though the figure is only very approximate. By the early 1950s probably less than 10% of the men being ordained were calling themselves Evangelicals. Again this figure is an uncertain one but only two theological colleges (Tyndale Hall in Bristol and Oak Hill in London) were producing ordinands who were, for all practical purposes, all in the Evangelical tradition.

At the end of the 1960s the Church Assembly commissioned a report on the state of the theological colleges. This was undertaken by the future Archbishop of Canterbury and the future

Bishop of Oxford (Kenneth Woollcombe) and was known as the 'Runcie Report'. For the first time the theological colleges were identified as being 'Tractarian', 'Evangelical' or 'Central'. Working on that basis the following figures, published by the General Synod's statistical unit, give a good indication on the remarkable transformation that has taken place. The figures relate only to full-time ordinands at the fourteen English theological colleges and omit those training through the various regional schemes whose loyalties are more difficult to identify.

Year	'Evangelical'	'Central'	'Tractarian'*	Total
1969	274 (31.2%)	347 (39.5%)	258 (29.3%)	879
1977	300 (44.7%)	273 (40.7%)	98 (14.6%)	671
1978	301 (44.2%)	254 (37.3%)	126 (18.5%)	681
1983	348 (47.3%)	264 (35.9%)	123 (16.8%)	735
1984	340 (48.0%)	245 (34.5%)	124 (17.5%)	709
1985	357 (49.0%)	240 (33.0%)	131 (18.0%)	728
1986	407 (51.6%)	246 (31.2%)	136 (17.2%)	789

*These figures do not include those for Ripon College, Cuddesdon. Ripon Hall was, before its merger with Cuddesdon, a 'Central' College. Cuddesdon was 'Tractarian'. The 'Tractarian' column above should therefore probably be increased from 1976 onwards and the 'Central' figures reduced accordingly. No actual figures of these proportions are available. The total of 'Evangelical' numbers is not thereby affected.

Obviously the most significant single point demonstrated by these figures is the rise in ordinands in the Evangelical colleges in the seventeen years 1969–1986 from 31% to 51% of those in full-time training. When to this is added the more uncertain figure of about 10% in the early 1950s the growth is almost phenomenal. From a tiny minority to what is, by some way, the largest group of ordinands, (now a majority of those in full-time training) is probably the most important growth statistic of all as regards Anglican Evangelical development in the forty years since the end of the Second World War. Of course all figures of this kind must be treated with care since not every ordinand can be automatically identified with the stance of his theological college. Nevertheless, allowing for marginal variations, the main thrust of the figures is irresistible and if the trend continues for even one more decade the numerical position will place Anglican Evangelicals very firmly in the driving seat of the Church of England – at any rate as regards their numbers of clergy. When to these figures are attached the expectations of retirements within the next ten years – something between 1,700 and 3,000 men, many of whom come from the era when Evangelicals being ordained were below a quarter – the consequences are inescapable.

For the present, out of 10,750 working clergy in the Church of England approximately 3000 are regarded by the leading Anglican Evangelical society as being definitely identified with the movement. This does not include the not-inconsiderable number who, since the rise of the charismatic movement in the late 1960s, have preferred not to use any of the traditional 'labels' but whose training, background, and convictions have given them sympathies, with regard to the Bible and Christian doctrine, which are generally in the range which might be considered broadly Evangelical.

It is when one begins to look at the third area – the make-up of the hierarchy of the Church of England – that the discrepancy between Evangelical numbers, and their representation at senior diocesan levels, becomes visibly acute. Once again, it is difficult to be precise but if one considers Evangelicals to be those who have openly identified themselves with the 'Keele and Nottingham tradition' the figures can be quoted with some confidence. Below, then, are statistics calculated on that basis and, where some doubt exists, interpretation has been based on a more generous (rather than a less generous) use of the word. The figures are calculated on the situation pertaining in April 1987 and only attempt to identify Evangelical clergy holding senior offices. Vacancies are not included but announced preferments are.

Office	Totals	Evangelicals	Percentage
Diocesan Bishops	44	7	15.9%
Suffragan Bishops	63	7	11.1%
Deans and Provosts	42	3	7.1%
Archdeacons	109	13	11.9%
Totals	258	30	11.6%

The figures which most disturb Evangelicals are those recorded for archdeacons and (especially) suffragan bishops. Why these? Because, to put it simply, in recent years appointments to diocesan bishop have mostly been drawn from those already in suffragan sees. In Canterbury province, for example, there have been 21 diocesan appointments since 1980 and 16 of these have been from existing suffragans. But who appoints suffragans? Unlike the diocesans there is no influence exerted by the Crown or the Crown Appointments

Commission. The suffragans are appointed by their diocesans presumably in consultation with the Archbishop concerned. The present system strongly militates against the appointment of Evangelical suffragans (seven out of sixty-three) and makes it substantially harder for men to gain episcopal experience increasingly required in those to be appointed diocesans. A somewhat similar situation exists with regard to archdeacons.

It is not within the scope of this book to attempt to assess the reasons for the huge discrepancy between the percentages of Evangelical clergy working within the Church of England's ministry and those appointed to be the leaders. Nevertheless, it continues to be a cause for dissatisfied comment in Evangelical parishes across the country that they produce the men and a disproportionately high level of financial support for the Church of England only to see a mere handful preferred to leadership.

Ecclesiastical influence

While it is true that Anglican Evangelical clergy are still numerically seriously under-represented at the level of the hierarchy, the growth of Evangelical influence in the major policy-making national church bodies has been very considerable. Much of this has taken place since the Keele Congress of 1967 and this is perhaps a convenient place in which to record that remarkable event.

'In 1956', wrote George Hoffman in an article covering the publication of the Keele Statement, 'the Rev. Raymond Turvey was appointed Vicar of St. George's, Leeds. Before long he sensed a feeling of loneliness and isolation among many clergy, including Evangelicals, and began to arrange small informal gatherings of thirty or forty ministers at a time, for discussion, study and fellowship. Within four years these meetings for ministers had grown into the first Northern Evangelical Conference, held at York, and drawing 250 clergy from all over the Northern province. A highly successful layman's conference was held in Leeds in 1964, and the following year came the second Northern Conference, again at York'.[78]

'However', Hoffman continued, 'there was still a sense in which Northern Evangelicals felt that too many initiatives of evangelical thought and action tended to stem from London, and in consequence the idea developed of expanding the Northern Conference into a National Congress. This was the background to *Keele '67*, and NEAC, as it became affectionately known, began to take shape'.[79]

Hoffman went on to explain how in May 1964 a small group (John Stott, Peter Johnston, and John Goss) met with representatives of the Northern group. It was agreed to plan a National Evangelical Anglican Congress (NEAC) for April 1967 and, in due course, the campus of Keele University in Staffordshire was chosen as the site. John Stott, invited to become chairman, and Raymond Turvey, secretary, together with others, became the organising committee. This committee sought, and received, the backing of the Church of England Evangelical Council (still in its infancy); the Church Pastoral-Aid Society, the Church Society, the Fellowship of Evangelical Churchmen and the Federation of Diocesan Evangelical Unions. From the beginning, the Congress had in mind the Lambeth Conference of 1968 and its themes of renewal of the faith and ministry of the Church and Christian unity were to be well covered in the Keele Congress and in its Report.

In the years immediately before the Congress three other conferences took place which were all to play their part in what transpired at Keele. The first gathering, the British Council of Churches 'Faith and Order' conference, took place at Nottingham University in September 1964 and, thanks to the good offices of Canon David Paton of the Missionary and Ecumenical Council of the Church Assembly (MECCA), I was invited to attend as an official Anglican delegate (since I was about to take up the post of Secretary of the Liverpool Council of Churches – the first Evangelical clergyman to hold such an ecumenical office in an English city). That was the conference at which the famous 'Unity by Easter 1980' motion was passed and I was glad to be able to vote for it. The number of Anglican Evangelical clergy present could be counted on the fingers of one hand, indeed I can only recall the names of Canon A. T. Houghton (one of the speakers), Colin Scott (now Bishop of Hulme), and myself. Nevertheless Nottingham 1964 contributed one very crucial ingredient to NEAC of which more anon. The second, called 'Facing the Future', took place at The Hayes, Swanwick, in Derbyshire. I and a number of Eclectics were present and we were not at all happy with the diet put before us. A small group of us met in the middle of the night and a habit formed which had considerable consequences for the future.

The third conference held in late October 1966 was the annual Eclectic Society gathering, also at Swanwick. Once again the late night agitators got together and, well after one in the morning we agreed to put a proposal before the conference in plenary, on the next, final, morning. Our anxiety, and therefore our plan, stemmed from the rumour that Keele was going to subject a thousand delegates to nine, hour-long, addresses and that would be the Congress – full stop! To the Eclectics, all in our mid-thirties, this was an intolerable prospect and we, the late-night Young Turks, were out, if there was still time, to fight the idea tooth and nail. Who were we? George Hoffman, Gavin Reid, Frank Entwistle, Eddie Shirras, Philip Crowe and myself. Bouncing up and down on the floor in mini-sleeping bags were my twin daughters, aged 20 months, as my wife Jackie tried to keep them and us in order and get us all to bed! I doubt if the book-room at Swanwick has ever seen such a gathering at getting on for two o'clock at night, or one of such potential consequences.

My own contribution was to stress the absolute necessity of a major Statement (I got that from the Faith and Order conference) and together we decided to press for that and for the pre-publication of the Congress addresses in book form so that the bulk of the time might be given to discussion and the preparation of a Statement in final form, based on the circulation of a draft Statement in advance.

Next day the Eclectics plenary endorsed our proposals and Gavin Reid took them to the next meeting of the Congress committee. Peter Johnston, Vicar of Islington, immediately reacted by saying 'I feel a sense of relief' and the changes were adopted. Unknown to all but Gavin Reid, John King, editor of the *Church of England Newspaper*, was pacing up and down outside, amid flurries of snow, praying desperately that the committee would accept the proposals. His prayers were more than answered! George Hoffman, Philip Crowe, John Simpson and myself were appointed to the committee and the new wave had arrived with a vengeance. We never looked back. A 'Statement' group was set up, under Dr Jim Packer, which included Colin Buchanan, Michael Green, Gavin Reid and Philip Crowe. I became Congress Press Officer and also Secretary for Observers.

In the event it was the fact of the Congress and the nature of its Statement which made such enormous and immediate impact on the Church of England. Opened by the Archbishop of Canterbury, Dr Michael Ramsey, (whose Radio and Television Officer, six months later, I was to become) and closed by Stuart Blanch, Bishop of Liverpool (later to be Archbishop of York), it captured the imagination, not only of those present but also of Christian leaders across the country. It was, in the words of Sir John Lawrence, a member of the Church Assembly, 'a turning point for the whole church … I have been praying for something like NEAC for ten years'.[80] Sir Kenneth Grubb, Chairman of the Church Assembly's House of Laity, declared that Keele 'has done three remarkable things. It has given Evangelicals a justified sense of their standing; it has emphasized their loyalty to the Church; it has demonstrated that they have much to contribute, not only to individual faith, but also to the great spiritual challenges of contemporary society. Can one expect more?'[81]

Keele was especially a personal triumph for John Stott and Norman Anderson, both of whom chaired sub-plenaries of 500 people in the final approval stage of the Statement. On a purely personal note, I felt like King Midas. Absolutely everything I touched turned to gold! I dare say that all the committee felt much the same. Randle Manwaring sums Keele up in one pithy sentence: 'There had never been anything remotely like it before'. It was, he added, 'perhaps the most significant evangelical landmark in twentieth-century Anglicanism'.[82]

What in essence did Keele say? Certainly it said nothing new in the doctrinal field. Nor were its remarks about Mission, the World, and Church Structures particularly striking. What caught the eye were its statements about liturgical revision ('the period of experiment is welcome ... liturgical revision is long overdue'); the gospel sacraments ('indiscriminate infant baptism ... is a scandal' and 'we determine to work towards the ... weekly celebration of the sacrament as the central corporate service of the church') and ecumenical relations ('we are no longer content to stand apart from those with whom we disagree' since all Trinitarian Christians 'have a right to be treated as Christians').[83]

These, and the ringing affirmation that Anglican Evangelicals were 'deeply committed to the present and future of the Church of England' left no-one in any doubt that the new generation was genuinely part of the Church of England and seeking its reform in a manner entirely free from the kind of sectarian spirit that had too often characterised the movement in the past.

The message was heard, inside and outside the Evangelical world, and the transformation which had been going on for over a decade suddenly burst upon the Church of England. Almost at once Anglican Evangelicals found themselves becoming 'flavour of the month'. They began to be appointed to committees and commissions. My own appointment to a Church House post followed soon after and I was told quite plainly (in due course) that it was because of what had happened at Keele. A new era had quite evidently begun.

Since 1967, Anglican Evangelicals – clerical and lay – have found themselves growing stronger in influence almost every year. At the level of diocesan bishops they moved from virtually none (all the earlier ones had been 'liberal' Evangelicals, of whom Archbishop Michael Ramsey once said that 'they would never stand up and be counted') to seven by 1987 (out of forty four). As has already been noted their representation at the other levels of the hierarchy is derisory.

Within the General Synod there are, in 1987, roughly sixty in the House of Clergy (as compared with about thirty-five in 1975) and one hundred and ten in the House of Laity. On the Synod's Standing Committee, of eight elected clergy there are three and of elected laity (eight) there are four. The impact of these numbers is diminished by the number of *ex officio* members (twelve), of whom only two are Evangelicals. From 1970 to 1979 the Chairman of the House of Laity was Sir Norman Anderson while, since 1985 Mrs Jill Dann has been Vice Chairman. Anderson's predecessor, Sir Kenneth Grubb, was also an Evangelical. Archdeacon Peter Dawes has played a very significant role as Chairman of the Business Sub-Committee.

As regards the Church Commissioners, of the total number of ninety-six, forty-four are *ex officio* (being diocesan bishops) and fourteen are appointed by the Queen, the Archbishop of Canterbury, and others. Ten are political appointees, in office by virtue of their government position (such as the Prime Minister, Home Secretary, Lord Chancellor, Chancellor of the Exchequer, Lord Chief Justice, and so on). Of the remaining twenty-eight, twenty-five are elected by the General Synod. The House of Laity elects ten, of whom at least five are Evangelicals. The House of Clergy elects ten, of whom at least four are Evangelicals, while of the five elected by the Cathedral deans and provosts none are Evangelicals. Since, in practice, the 'working' Commissioners number about forty-five it can be seen that nine of these are Evangelicals. It must however be stressed that issues directly involving questions of churchmanship are very rarely met in the Church Commissioners committees or indeed on the Board of Governors, numbering twenty-nine, of whom six are Evangelicals. Nevertheless, the numerical growth again speaks for itself.

Evangelical General Synod members serve as members (usually in a minority) on all the major Synod Boards and Councils. The Chairman of the Board for Mission and Unity; the Chairman of the Faith and Order Advisory Group; the Vice-Chairman of the Board for Social Responsibility; the Chairman and Deputy-Vice-Chairman of the Pensions Board – all these are Evangelicals. Evangelicals also serve on the Doctrine, Liturgical, and Dioceses Commissions. Among staff executives, top posts in the Central Board of Finance, the Advisory Council for the Church's Ministry, and the Board for Social Responsibility have all, in recent years, been held by Evangelicals – lay or clerical. Others have been in charge of Women's Ministry, Radio and Television, and within the Board of Mission and Unity. Almost half the newly-selected Church Urban Fund Trustees are Evangelicals. Only in the Board for Education has no senior appointment been made in the seventeen years since synodical government began. It is also worth noting that many of the 'under 30s' and black members of the General Synod are Evangelicals.

Finally, of the eight clerical and lay members elected by the General Synod to the Crown Appointments Commission, two have been Evangelicals in the ten years since its inception, Jill Dann since 1977 and Colin Craston since 1982. Evangelicals have also been members of the Anglican Consultative Council (Colin Craston being Vice-Chairman), members of the British Council of Churches and official delegates to the World Council of Churches assemblies. Outside the central structures, there have been a significant number of lay chairmen of diocesan Synods.

None of these figures prove that the men and women concerned have been effective. That is a matter for others to decide. What, however, they do show is that Evangelicals and especially lay Evangelicals, given the opportunity to play their full role in the Church of England in the last twenty years, have not been slow to do so. They have demonstrated conclusively that Keele's claim to be 'deeply committed to the Church of England' was no idle boast. They have, moreover, gone a long way towards answering David Paton's post-Keele enquiry as to whether 'Evangelicals have fully grasped that to play a real part in the corporate life of the Church of England involves taking very seriously (positively as well as negatively) the existence and views of those in the Church of England who are not' of their persuasion.[84] It is a plain fact that in the past twenty years it has not generally been the Evangelicals who have blocked and frustrated the will of the majority on issue after issue. Only very rarely have Evangelicals, in these two decades, taken up a negative stance and then it has, without exception, been on issues where they believed that essential theological and ethical matters were being compromised.

Theological development

One of the most widespread popular misunderstandings about the Evangelical movement is the assumption made by many that 'Evangelical' is merely a synonym for 'keen on Evangelism'. On that assumption, many whose basic attitudes to the Christian faith are far from biblical claim to be 'Evangelical' simply because they claim to be in favour of telling other people about the Christian faith in some form or other. It cannot be stressed too strongly that Evangelical Christianity 'is theological in its character and biblical in its substance'. In short, it is rooted and grounded in a framework of convictions which find their origin in, and take their framework from, the Bible. Evangelism, on the other hand, is often wrongly perceived to be merely another word for propaganda. Thus the *Independent* newspaper can speak of an 'American anti-tobacco evangelist' on an 'evangelising mission to Britain'.[85] This, to most Christians, is an offensive misuse of a word which speaks not of propaganda techniques but of the 'evangel' (a New Testament Greek word meaning 'good news of the Kingdom of God'). So to be involved in Evangelism is to be specifically engaged in proclaiming the good news as it is to be found in the Bible, and supremely in the teaching of Jesus and his apostles. Thus, an Evangelical is one whose beliefs are shaped by the same teaching and who, in proclaiming it, is called to a ministry of Evangelism. Yet by no means all Evangelicals are effective Evangelists and not all who try to be Evangelists are necessarily Evangelicals.

Evangelical belief is, then, a coherent pattern of doctrinal material drawn from, and consistent with, Holy Scripture. It is, in that sense, a 'theology' and it stands over against other theologies whose basic shape is not primarily determined by the Scriptural revelation but by other extraneous forces. For example, 'Catholic theology' takes its starting point from Scripture but moves well beyond (and, as Evangelicals argue, is often contrary to) Scripture, by the way in which it allows the historical development of ideas and practices to determine the place which Scripture ultimately has within its contemporary formulation. In a more extreme form, 'Liberal theology' only pays lip service to Scripture, using it only when it happens to agree with the current fashions of thought in any given era but happily jettisoning it when it reaches contrary conclusions to those of the gurus of the decade. The jaundiced but accurate death blow to Liberalism was delivered by Dean Inge long ago when he declared that 'he who marries the spirit of the age is soon widowed'.

Such a criticism does not exonerate an Evangelical from carefully listening to, and assessing, the philosophies of each age, but it does warn him not to be swamped by their often meretricious surface attractions.

In common with Roman Catholics, Evangelicals 'are entirely agreed on the necessity of revelation, if human beings are ever to know God'. This statement opens the Report of the Evangelical – Roman Catholic Dialogue on Mission, published in 1986. The Report continues 'we are agreed that since the biblical texts have been inspired by God, they remain the ultimate, permanent and normative reference to the revelation of God. To them the church must continually return' and adds that 'what the human authors wrote is what God intended should be revealed, and thus that Scripture is without error'. To the question 'are human words adequate to describe God fully?' the answer is given 'not ... fully', but 'they do reveal him truly'.[86]

This attitude to Scripture is, without doubt, the one which governed virtually all Christian thinking before the past two centuries. It was not until the ironically-entitled 'Enlightenment' that first unbelievers, and later, Liberal Christians began to accept agnostic pre-suppositions which came, as the influence of the churches declined, to dominate the thinking of educated men and women in Western Europe. That more and more educated men and women are beginning to reject its presuppositions and reconsider the older Christian claim to a unique divine revelation expressed in Scripture and that this rejection is to be found among both Roman Catholics and Evangelicals, is clearly a matter for consideration. It would have been hard, eighty years ago, to prophesy that as Evangelicals became better educated they increasingly would find themselves unpersuaded by the Liberal certainties which dominated their own education, not least in the Theology faculties of the universities. Here, at least, it may be true that 'Karl Barth strikes again'.

However, as far as Anglican Evangelicals are concerned, it is not the doctrine of revelation which has been supreme in their recent thinking, since they mostly take it for granted as being quite consistent with their belief in God the Holy Trinity.

What has been one of the chief Evangelical theological interests for the past decade has been the continuing debate on hermeneutics. This came to the fore at the 1977 Nottingham Congress ('son of Keele') when Dr Anthony Thiselton placed the subject firmly on the Evangelicals' agenda. Dr Thiselton, then a lecturer in Biblical Studies at Sheffield University and now Principal of St John's College, Nottingham, propounded ten theses which recognised the need for 'careful investigation of the Bible's 'linguistic, historical, literary and theological context and its setting in the ancient world'; the historical conditioning of the modern reader which demands a proper 'historical distancing' before any application is attempted; the need for 'a fusion between two sets of horizons, namely those of the text and those of the modern reader'; and the avoidance of the kind of 'appeal to the doctrine of the Spirit' which might seem to 'relieve Christians of the responsibility to take these hermeneutical issues seriously'.[87]

This relationship between a strong doctrine of revelation in Scripture and the need for a sophisticated hermeneutic by which to expound and apply its contents seems well calculated to meet the balance required in the modern Preface to the Declaration of Assent as used at Institutions, Licensing and the Consecration of Bishops, in which the Church of England 'professes the faith uniquely revealed in the Holy Scriptures ... which faith the Church is called upon to proclaim afresh in each generation'.[88]

Such a combination of the 'given' and its proper exposition, puts the contemporary Evangelical Anglican (supposing he takes both seriously) into a completely different world from that of the Fundamentalist. To the latter, what 'the Bible says' is all that matters and its application is no more than the wooden repetition of the words, whatever the circumstances. Such an exposition is no longer acceptable to most thinking Anglican Evangelicals and this has led to a division of opinion on the subject of the ordination of women.

This particular development is only one of those which have affected the movement in the past thirty-five years. In that period the level of Evangelical scholarship – inside and outside the Church of England – has consistently advanced. Doctorates – a rare commodity in the 1940s – have become a fact of life and university teaching posts are no longer regarded as unattainable or closed to those of biblically conservative convictions. In all this, the hopes of the Biblical Research Committee, back in the 1930s, have continued to be fulfilled. As this has happened, especially in the three related fields of biblical scholarship, dogmatic theology, and philosophy, tensions have arisen which have led to a very healthy controversy. The dogmatic theologians, such as James Packer, have been properly anxious to safeguard the doctrines of biblical inspiration and authority; the biblical scholars, such as

James Dunn, have struggled to maintain a proper critical honesty concerning the actual documents, while the philosophers, such as Anthony Thiselton, have pressed the need for a careful hermeneutic in the exegesis, exposition and application of the sacred text. The Anglican Evangelical movement is in debt to each group not least because all are needed in the work of effectively educating the mass of relatively illiterate Christians in the pews who are often tempted to look for a package of easy answers. That problem is by no means limited to those in the Evangelical tradition!

It might be helpful at this point to refer to the recently published Basis of Faith of the Church of England Evangelical Council. Historically, Evangelicals have been people who value a written framework through which the essentials of the Faith are conserved and passed on from generation to generation. Thus they continue to value the Thirty Nine Articles of Religion (published in 1571) much more highly than most other Anglicans. Early in the twentieth century various attempts were made by interdenominational bodies to produce their own Bases of Faith. Most of these were constructed without reference to ecclesiological or sacramental doctrines though the Basis of the Bible Churchmen's Missionary Society did incorporate certain clauses which especially reflected the conflicts of the early 1920s within the Church of England.

Early in the 1960s a short Basis was framed by the founders of the Evangelical Fellowship in the Anglican Communion (EFAC) and this, a fairly minimal statement, served to give some specific doctrinal coherence to Evangelicals in the growing number of Provinces throughout the Anglican Communion. The Basis did however have one or two glaring weaknesses and omissions and when, in 1983, the new Anglican Evangelical Assembly first met in London and adopted the EFAC Basis, I gave notice that I intended to work for a new and greatly improved Basis to be adopted at the earliest opportunity. In 1984 the Assembly agreed to set in motion the machinery to bring this about. Later that year, a Working Party, chaired by Gordon Landreth, and consisting of Dr John Webster, Roger Beckwith and myself, was set up by the Assembly's Standing Committee (the Church of England Evangelical Council). I prepared a first draft which was altered and augmented and, in due course, accepted by a near-unanimous vote at the 1986 Assembly. The Basis, which follows a novel framework, is now therefore the most up-to-date statement of the essential beliefs held by Anglican Evangelicals in England. It reads as follows:[89]

1. *Introduction*
   As members of the Church of England within the one, holy, catholic and apostolic church we *affirm* the faith uniquely revealed in the holy Scriptures and set forth in the catholic creeds, of which faith the Thirty Nine Articles of Religion are a general exposition. Standing in the Reformation tradition we lay especial emphasis on the grace of God – his unmerited mercy – as expressed in the doctrines which follow.

2. *God as the Source of Grace*
   In continuity with the teaching of holy Scripture and the Christian creeds, *we worship* one God in three Persons – Father, Son, and Holy Spirit. God has created all things, and us in his own image; all life, truth, holiness, and beauty come from him. His Son Jesus Christ, fully God and fully man, was conceived through the Holy Spirit and born of the Virgin Mary, was crucified, died, rose and ascended to reign in glory.

3. *The Bible as the Revelation of Grace*
   We receive the canonical books of the Old and New Testaments as the wholly reliable revelation and record of God's grace, given by the Holy Spirit as the true word of God written. The Bible has been given to lead us to salvation, to be the ultimate rule for Christian faith and conduct, and the supreme authority by which the Church must ever reform itself and judge its traditions.

4. *The Atonement as the Work of Grace*
   We believe that Jesus Christ came to save lost sinners. Though sinless, he bore our sins, and their judgment, on the cross, thus accomplishing our salvation. By raising Christ bodily from the dead, God vindicated him as Lord and Saviour and proclaimed his victory. Salvation is in Christ alone.

5. *The Church as the Community of Grace*
   We hold that the Church is God's covenant community, whose members, drawn from every nation, having been justified by grace through faith, inherit the promises made to Abraham and fulfilled in Christ. As a fellowship of the Spirit manifesting his fruit and exercising his gifts, it is called to worship God, grow in grace, and bear witness to him and his Kingdom. God's Church is one body and must ever strive to discover and experience that unity in truth and love which it has in Christ, especially through its confession of the apostolic faith and in its observance of the dominical Sacraments.

6. *The Sacraments as the Signs of Grace*
   We maintain that the Sacraments of Baptism and Holy Communion

proclaim the gospel as effective and visible signs of our justification and sanctification, and as true means of God's grace to those who repent and believe. Baptism is the sign of forgiveness of sin, the gift of the Spirit, new birth to righteousness and entry into the fellowship of the People of God. Holy Communion is the sign of the living, nourishing presence of Christ through his Spirit to his people; the memorial of his one, perfect, completed and all-sufficient sacrifice for sin, from whose achievement all may benefit but in whose offering none can share; and an expression of our corporate life of sacrificial thanksgiving and service.

7. *Ministry as the Stewardship of Grace*
   We share, as the people of God, in a royal priesthood common to the whole Church, and in the community of the Suffering Servant. Our mission is the proclamation of the gospel by the preaching of the word, as well as by caring for the needy, challenging evil and promoting justice and a more responsible use of the world's resources. It is the particular vocation of bishops and presbyters, together with deacons, to build up the body of Christ in truth and love, as pastors, teachers, and servants of the servants of God.

8. *Christ's Return as the Triumph of Grace*
   We look forward expectantly to the final manifestation of Christ's grace and glory when he comes again to raise the dead, judge the world, vindicate his chosen and bring his Kingdom to its eternal fulfilment in the new heaven and the new earth.

It will be seen that the Basis indicates the movement's convictions on the kind of theological issues raised in recent years by David Jenkins, Bishop of Durham. While not directly attempting to defend the doctrines under attack the Basis maintains the historic beliefs in the virginal conception of Our Lord Jesus by the operation of the Holy Spirit and the willing response of his mother, Mary. It also defines the resurrection of Jesus as having been a bodily act the purpose of which was the vindication of Christ by his Father.

Other doctrines emphasised are the creative activity of God; the divine image in man; the purpose of the Bible; the vicarious, substitutionary, death of Christ; the Church as a covenant community rooted in the promise of Abraham; the ecumenical task of that community; the sacraments as effective signs of justification and sanctification; the relationship between Christ's death and the eucharistic action; the role of the threefold order of ministry within the royal priesthood of the whole Church; and the ultimate fulfilment of Christ's coming Kingdom as he returns to complete his work. Integrating all is the grace of God.

Here then is where Anglican Evangelicals stand, as regards their essential theology. To be an Anglican Evangelical is to hold to these beliefs (or something closely akin to them). They are, in essence, the same beliefs as animated the Church of England at the Reformation. It is certainly arguable that they represent the apostolic doctrines 'uniquely revealed in the holy Scriptures and set forth in the catholic creeds, which faith the Church is called upon to proclaim afresh in each generation'. These are the truths, Evangelicals believe, which our world needs to hear confidently, yet sensitively, proclaimed by the Church of England.

Liturgical advance

If there was one thing which could be said with absolute confidence in the 1940s it was that Evangelicals for the most part, knew nothing about liturgy and cared even less. They had, if they were ordinands, done the necessary lectures and swotted up the essential parts of Neil and Willoughby's *Tutorial Prayer Book* in order to counter the views expressed by Proctor and Frere. They knew their Prayer Books and used the 1662 book with hardly a thought for the illegal alternatives suggested by the 1928 book. Sunday by Sunday at 8 a.m. they used the 1662 Holy Communion, wearing scarf, hood and surplice and standing at the North 'Side' (though in practice it was 'End'). Then at 11 and 6.30 they used Morning and Evening Prayer (never called Mattins and Evensong) and perhaps once a month 'tacked on' a bit of Holy Communion (starting from 'Ye that do truly') for the few who stayed behind. At 4 o'clock they did Infant Baptisms (often with very uneasy consciences) for all who turned up. If they could avoid it (and usually they could) they declined to turn East for the Creed. That was the liturgy as they used it and anyone who did anything else was highly suspect. Laymen usually read lessons (dressed in dark suits) and laywomen stayed in their pews. Children, for the most part, were not present as they were next door at the Sunday school. In many Evangelical churches the really 'keen' (a much-used 'in' word) came to the Sunday evening, rather than the Sunday morning, service.

That, by and large, continued to be the situation until well into the 1960s. When, in 1961, as a Curate at Edgware Parish Church I produced a very slightly doctored version of Evening Prayer for an

Evangelistic Service (with my Rector, Gordon Harman's, approval) I received requests for copies from all over the world, on average once every ten days for eighteen months. My 'doctored' version was, of course, strictly illegal but by then the first signs of a desire for something just a little more modern than Cranmer's deathless prose were beginning to be evident. In the same year, in a weekly column which I wrote for the *Church of England Newspaper* under the pseudonym 'Qoheleth', I floated the idea of taking the Westward Position (facing the congregation) at Holy Communion. Apart from William Leathem, who was doing it at Harborne, in Birmingham, no Evangelical parish clergyman dared to say such at thing, let alone do it, for fear of being blackballed from the patronage lists. When I first actually did it, at a weekend houseparty conference at Stoke Poges in 1962, I eyed the sky cautiously, awaiting Divine Retribution. Meanwhile, back at the ranch at Edgware, we built a new daughter church, specially set up for Westward-facing Communion. Not until Keele in 1967 did Evangelicals publicly 'commend consideration of the Westward position'.[90] Some even today, have still never ceased using 'North Side' with a Holy Table up against the East wall of their churches in, ironically, the position ordered by Archbishop Laud in his reaction against the Puritans.

Evangelicals were certainly perceived by the rest of the Church of England as being absolutely hostile to liturgical change. The most famous, and most hostile, statement to this effect was made in 1945 by Dom Gregory Dix. Evangelicals were, he argued, 'permanently impenetrable behind a financial rampart to any ideas current in the rest of the church'. They would, he added, 'offer the most determined and conscientious opposition' to the framing 'of any new liturgy' and would 'certainly decline to use it'. This fact would not, however, 'prevent their obstructing the official compilation of any new rite'.[91] Colin Buchanan, himself the most able liturgical scholar produced by the Evangelicals, probably since Cranmer, acknowledged, in 1984, that, given Dix's perspectives in 1945 there was 'an element of sheer truth about this'.[92] Even as late as 1958 Evangelical leaders were seeing liturgical revision as a threat and although, by Keele, it was acknowledged that 'liturgical revision is long overdue' and many welcoming noises were made about the services beginning to come from the hands of the Liturgical Commission, the note of fear was still evident. There were 'serious objections' to some of the proposed services. Flaws were detected in Confirmation, the Burial service and the Holy Communion – all Series Two – and second and third century practices were frowned on as not offering a proper basis for liturgical revision. Nevertheless 'the period of experiment' was 'welcome' and the fact that Evangelicals had a record of being 'suspicious of experimentation and frightened of change' was openly admitted.

What caused the change between 1958 and 1967? It would seem that two factors were at work. On the one hand younger clergy in the Eclectic Society were anxious to see some modern alternatives available to set alongside the 1662 Prayer Book for purely pastoral reasons.

The other, and far more important factor, was the result of a letter sent by John Wenham, who years before had been one of the founders of the Biblical Research Committee, to Archbishops Ramsey and Coggan. In it he argued that the Evangelical opposition to change was not a matter of principle but a reaction to their complete exclusion from all the official commissions from which proposals for change came. Colin Buchanan describes the Archbishops' sympathetic response as possibly having been 'a crisis moment in the life of Church of England'.[93] One result was an invitation to Buchanan from Archbishop Michael Ramsey to serve on the Liturgical Commission. Buchanan had only been ordained in 1961 and was a mere thirty-one years old. He had however achieved the distinction of having secured a 100% mark for liturgy in his General Ordination Examination papers. He has told the story of what happened next in his Grove Booklet, *Evangelical Anglicans and Liturgy*, published years later as *Tract Ninety* in the Grove Worship series. In the sixteen years which followed, culminating in the arrival of the Alternative Service Book of 1980, Colin Buchanan grew to become a towering figure in the field of Anglican liturgy. Almost single-handed, he converted the Evangelicals from being liturgical cave men into being enthusiastic experimenters, out in the vanguard in the late 1970s and early 1980s. From a group which he gathered around himself came a stream of booklets on liturgical subjects which still flows after twelve years of regular publication. This reached a high point with the issuing in 1980 of the lavishly illustrated and very popular *Anglican Worship Today* whose arrival coincided with the printing of the Alternative Service Book. Almost all of its fifteen contributors were Anglican Evangelical clergy.

One other important decision affecting Evangelical responses to liturgical change came with the final stages of the revision of the Series Three Holy Communion Service in 1978. Up to that point no service had managed to contain a Eucharistic prayer acceptable to the whole Church. Indeed it was widely assumed that it simply was not possible to frame an 'anamnesis' (the crucial, controversial, heart of the prayer) that could satisfy both Evangelicals and Anglo-Catholics. The General Synod Standing Committee, in a moment of mad rashness, appointed a Revision Committee, chaired by Cyril Bowles, Bishop of Derby, (an older-generation Liberal Evangelical) with fourteen members, seven being Anglo-Catholic and seven Evangelical. There were, as one irreverent wag put it, 'fourteen scorpions in a bottle'. Over a thousand textual amendments were submitted to the Revision Committee, which was a very relaxed and happy group of people (I know, I was one of the 'scorpions'), and to the amazement of almost everyone not only one, but four, Eucharistic prayers were prepared which all fourteen were prepared to commend and use. An impasse lasting almost one hundred and fifty years was removed and 'Rite A' as it became known is now used in thousands of English parishes of almost all traditions.

It is true that a small group of Evangelicals resisted Rite A on the grounds that it was '1928 all over again'. In this they failed to note a number of highly significant differences. First, the whole liturgical background had changed. The influence of the Liturgical Movement, the adoption of Westward position behind a free-standing Holy Table, the widespread use of modern eucharistic vestments specifically and canonically denuded of 'doctrinal significance' – all these provided a setting in which certain words, used in a modified form, became acceptable to most Evangelicals. For example, in Rite A the epiclesis (prayer to the Holy Spirit) was not couched in 'bless and sanctify these gifts' terms but rather as a prayer that 'They may be to us his body and his blood'. So, too, the oblationary language in which the consecrated elements were 'offered' to God was carefully modified and used only 'this sacrifice of praise and thanksgiving'. In its place, words like 'celebrate' and 'make the memorial', (which were much less divisive) were agreed upon. As a result, many Anglicans gladly laid the ghosts of 1927–28 to rest and Rite A has probably become more widely and enthusiastically used in Evangelical parishes than in those of any other tradition. Eat your heart out Gregory Dix

The growing use of Holy Communion in Evangelical parishes was a good example of the movement having taken note of those in other traditions, in this case from the Parish Communion supporters whose slogan was 'The Lord's People round the Lord's Table on the Lord's Day'. They in turn had been deeply influenced by the Continental Liturgical Movement, chiefly to be found among Roman Catholics in Germany, France, Holland, and Belgium. Some of the

Evangelicals had gone straight to them to see examples of their work while others were particularly challenged by Peter Hammond's *Liturgy and architecture*, published at the beginning of the 1960s. One of the prices which this movement had paid was the considerable reduction of preaching time and a survey which I conducted for *Prism* magazine showed that most parishes, other than Evangelical ones, had cut their only Sunday sermon down to an average of eight minutes. Archbishop Donald Coggan responded by quoting the warning that 'sermonettes make Christianettes' and the minimising of the preaching of Christian truth has been damaging to the Church of England ever since.

In three other ways Evangelicals have made a major contribution in the field of worship. It was they who pioneered the 'Family Service', a more informal service for young families which, while using some liturgical material, tended to incorporate choruses, quizzes, visual aids (especially by means of overhead projectors when these became available in the 1970s). Michael Botting led a group of Eclectics in the preparation of a suitable book, incorporating a service outline, modern hymns and choruses and contemporary prayers. The first draft of this was published in 1967 and by addressing God as 'you', became the first Anglican liturgical production to break away from the old 'thou' form. By 1971 the full book appeared, entitled *Family Worship* and was widely used, chiefly, but not exclusively, in Evangelical parishes. Botting published an extra book of suitable teaching material, *Teaching the Families*, in 1973. At much the same time, Dick Williams in Liverpool edited his first book of contemporary prayers which was drawn from a wide range of sources. In October 1986 a far more elaborate book, *Christian Family Worship*, was edited by Michael Perry, secretary of Jubilate Hymns, of whom more in a moment.

In the early 1960s a number of us who were curates with large youth groups set about producing our own local song and chorus books. At Reigate, Michael Baughen, now Bishop of Chester, published *Zing Sing*, a small collection, and together with Richard Bewes, later to be his successor at All Souls, Langham Place, edited *Youth Praise*, which contained 150 pieces, ranging from hymns, through songs and choruses, to items suitable for the multitude of Christian guitar groups which had sprung up. This was issued in 1966 and was followed by *Youth Praise Two* three years later, a second collection of the same size. New to this book was a very small selection of metrical psalms. The success of these triggered off a four-year project called *Psalm Praise* which, when issued in 1973, was premiered at large concerts across England in churches and in both Liverpool and Manchester cathedrals. *Psalm Praise* was entirely metrical and, generally, unrhymed, including versions of the Anglican canticles and about half the psalter. The book contained 151 pieces. Among the material used, a substantial amount of the music came from Norman Warren and David Wilson, both Evangelical clergy who have served in the General Synod. On the words side the bulk of the new pieces were written by Timothy Dudley-Smith, Michael Perry, Christopher Idle, Jim Seddon, Michael Baughen and myself. Literally hundreds of thousands of these three books have been used across the world.

An even more demanding and potentially much more controversial project was the preparation of *Hymns for Today's Church*. This took ten years and was edited by two teams – Words and Music – with Michael Baughen as consultant editor. I edited a Words team of nine and David Wilson a Music team of eight. We included new hymns, modern hymns and traditional hymns re-worded into 'you' language. Some other archaic words and phrases were also altered and the eucharistic hymns were adapted to fall within 'the reconciling tradition of the Church of England's Rite A order'. The book, while attracting hostile criticism (as expected) sold a quarter of a million copies in its first four years and is the only major book available for parishes seeking to use contemporary (i.e. 'you' form) liturgies, pew Bibles, and hymn books.

The third Evangelical contribution has been in the field of baptismal discipline. Back in the 1950s infant baptism was almost entirely indiscriminate in the way in which it was administered. Only a tiny handful of clergy were willing to carry the huge weight of public and ecclesiastical abuse which descended on those who attempted to practice a policy of discrimination. The best known of these was Christopher Wansey (not an Evangelical) who was totally uncompromising. In West Croydon, Philip Wood, an Evangelical of the small 'in between' tradition ordained at the beginning of the Second World War, followed Wansey's example. Baptisms were few and far between but were always conducted in the main Sunday services. During his Croydon incumbency, Wood had two curates, the first, Eddy Stride, who later made his name in the Church Assembly and General Synod, and myself. When, in 1972, I followed Michael Botting as the incumbent of St Matthew's Fulham, I found that he had adopted a similar policy which I naturally continued. Today, infant baptism is widely available in the country districts in an indiscriminate manner but in the towns, especially in the South East many, if not most parishes are much more careful in the choice of who should be baptised and when. Both Canon Law and the ASB service make much more in the way of demands upon both clergy and parents. Once again it was Evangelicals who helped to point the way forward. Both Keele in 1967 and the second NEAC at Nottingham in 1977 had strongly urged the Church of England to create 'a theologically-inspired national practice of baptismal discipline'[94] and when nothing was done, Nottingham called it 'a scandal'.[95]

It is sometimes argued that a stricter baptismal discipline is turning the Church of England in a Sectarian direction and that inevitable Church-State tensions will be exacerbated by the considerable reduction in infant baptisms which is the consequence. It is true that the percentage of infant baptisms has steadily declined in the past thirty years from about 60% in the 1950s to about 30% today. These range from about 15% in London diocese to 60% in Carlisle. In short, the more rural and conservative dioceses (Carlisle, Hereford and Lincoln) are still 'folk religion' orientated while the more urban and secularist (London, Southwark, Chelmsford and Birmingham) are under 25% and reflect the greater element of 'commitment or nothing' attitudes widely existing.

For Evangelicals the problem is sharpened by their own biblical 'covenant' theology which sees infant baptism as defensible only within the context of a worshipping Christian family. They have yet to discover any reputable biblical (or patristic) theology by which an 'open font' can be justified and were entirely unpersuaded by the only recent attempt, a book by R. R. Osborn, to supply a theology for what they regard as an indefensible practice. In this respect Anglican Evangelicals have been encouraged by the growing baptismal discipline emerging among Roman and Anglo-Catholics and by the report on 'Godparents', published in 1984 by Bishop Richard Rutt as a General Synod paper.[96] They are also glad to see their concern clearly endorsed by the World Council of Churches' 'Baptism, Eucharist and Ministry' document. They see their stand for a reputable pastoral discipline, applied gently but firmly, and with the option of a 'Thanksgiving' service being available where desired by parents, as having borne real fruit in the past twenty years.

As is widely known, the charismatic movement has made its impact across a very considerable range of churches and, within the Evangelical movement in the Church of England it has drawn out the full range of response from uncritical acceptance to hostility bordering on paranoia. Nevertheless the 'loosening up' process within both liturgical and non-liturgical worship has had its effect on many Evangelical churches. It was not, it must be noted, the only source of influence in the growth of informality but the fact that it has played a major part in that cannot be denied.

Parish church worship in the Evangelical tradition is, today, a radically different exercise in hundreds of parishes from what it was in the 1940s and 1950s. Gregory Dix has been proved to be completely mistaken. Arthur Couratin, from a similar tradition, made the same misjudgment when in the 1960s he told Colin Buchanan that 'Evangelicals will always have, and will always use, 1662'.[97] Today, it is precisely among the Evangelicals that the future of the Book of Common Prayer is so uncertain. Most of the bitter battles which have been fought in recent years concerning '1662 or ASB' have been fought in churches of a central tradition. Sometimes it is alleged that 'the colleges' (i.e. the theological colleges) are not using the old Prayer Book. The reverse is also, sometimes the case. I preached recently at an Oxford college in the Anglo-Catholic tradition (not a theological college) where some dons had never even seen an Alternative Service Book rite. They were living in a community claustrophobically bound up with the old liturgies. I found it ironical to think that the strictures pronounced by Dix and Couratin were being deserved by their own heirs in the middle 1980s! If you want to see lively liturgy conducted in a welcoming style then you could do worse than attend Anglican Evangelical worship today.

Parochial involvement

Many – not least among those who would personally distance themselves from the Evangelical movement – see the chief glory of its tradition as being its commitment to the parish system. Perhaps the main reason for this is, negatively, that for many years the parish was the only sphere open to Anglican Evangelical clergy. Not for them preferment to high office or even interest in such a possibility. Not for them university chaplaincies, service chaplaincies, diocesan specialist posts or even humble rural deaneries. If they were to stay in the Church of England then the parish it would have to be and, in any case, where better to reach the hearts of men, women and children?

The eighteenth century Evangelicals had, however, faced the problem of even humble parish preferment by the contacts which they forged with aristocratic patrons who had livings to fill. By Charles Simeon's time, the absolute necessity of securing continuing patronage had been met by the purchase of 'advowsons' – the legal right to appoint incumbents. Thus there came into being, dotted across England, parishes whose Evangelical tradition could be legally secured by right of patronage and thus some guarantee of consistency of teaching and worship. Such a continuity of 'churchmanship' has all too often been secured at the price of parochial eclecticism by which specific churches draw would-be worshippers from miles around. This undoubtedly produces, in well-known cases, Evangelical 'cathedrals' to which those disaffected with their own parish churches can travel and find security of belief, liturgical style, and fellowship. Such churches often draw many others, of 'Undenominational' outlook, who use them when in the vicinity and will, with a concern only for personal and family religion, quite happily go to churches and fellowships, of any denomination, which suit their outlook. Parochial eclecticism of this kind produces many ordinands and large church incomes. It also produces jealousy and hard feelings in what may be called non-Evangelical churches and in small and unfashionable Evangelical parishes, both of which see many of their most lively young people hiving off to join the exciting life, worship, and teaching at St Admirabilis-on-the-Mount.

By no means all Evangelical churches fall into this category and with the huge growth of Evangelical clergy in recent years many parish churches are not so much 'Evangelical churches' as 'churches with Evangelical ministry'. The latter often become the former when the new tradition takes deep hold upon a congregation and such a change can hardly be regarded as sinister so long as it happens in the natural course of events and not merely because a 'totalitarian' vicar has decreed the change. In fairness it should be added that such vicars are by no means characteristic of Evangelicalism or limited to it. A great many parish churches have been taken out and liturgically raped by clergy of quite different traditions! No one has a monopoly of such clergy.

There are, however, far more positive reasons for the development of an Evangelical tradition in a parish. Among these are a strong preaching and teaching ministry. Clergy and lay-people actively want to know and proclaim the great truths of the Faith as they are to be found, or rooted, in the Bible. Bible reading, Bible study, and Bible exposition are some of the glories of Evangelical people and they will spend time, money and effort in getting to grips with the great themes of Scripture. The stark challenge of the Bible reaches deep into those who want to be effective servants of Christ and shapes their convictions as well as opening their cheque-books. Thus Evangelical parishes produce a better than average proportion of theologically-informed and biblically-related people with a desire to take the gospel into the world at whatever cost. The outstanding record of 'missionary giving' in Evangelical churches is open for all to see. Thus, in return, they are fertilized by regular visits from Christians from other parts of the world – expatriates and nationals – and their outlook is accordingly expanded.

A second strong influence in Evangelical parishes is the active reality of committed praying. Evangelicals never 'say their prayers'. They pray. They do this both in their liturgical worship and in their practice of extempore praying. Sometimes this can be wearisome when long-winded 'saints' pour out the platitudinous 'language of Zion' but the majority simply get on with it, in groups or alone, and ask God in plain speech to work out his will in this situation and that. It can be a disturbing experience for those not used to it to find themselves in a group of adults who pray as if they expect God to be listening and who actually believe that he is going, in his good time, to do something in response. There is hardly a more potent influence on a person than the sight and sound of Christians who obviously reckon that the living God is plugged in to their wavelength. Of course there are obvious dangers built into such a praying life-style but they are not endemic to it and, wisely led, such prayer can be a transforming influence in a parish church.

One evident mark of many Evangelical congregations is the presence of a strong element of caring fellowship. The Church is the People of God and they are not merely an aggregate of individuals who turn up at the building at a certain regular time Sunday by Sunday. The Evangelistic impact of a welcoming, outward-looking, all-age fellowship of Christian people, who enjoy each other as a family (even when, like a family, they have the occasional quarrel) is clear enough. 'See how these Christians love one another', is no empty sneer in such situations.

A frequent characteristic of Evangelical churches has been the existence of lively children's and young people's activity. Prior to the 1960s, this tended to be either fostered by Sunday Schools or contacts with local, often independent, Bible classes and uniformed youth organisations, fed by the practice of non-worshipping parents sending their children (to get them out of the way?) on Sunday afternoons. The growing gulf in English society between church attendance and ordinary, and particularly, middle-class life-styles has substantially reduced that superficial contact and impact. Now, fewer children and young people are in the churches and the large majority of those who are, are the offspring of worshipping parents. Most of them are much more directly integrated into regular church Sunday worship and they are supported by a flourishing system of inter-related teaching groups which have the corporate acronym of CYPECS. Going downwards in age, these are CYFA (Church Youth Fellowships Association), Pathfinders, Explorers, Climbers, and Scramblers, all of which are under the aegis of the Church Pastoral-Aid Society. CP-AS provides a whole range of support for Evangelical churches and its effectiveness in providing modern literature, audio-visuals, camps and holiday 'ventures', together with a flourishing fellowship of ordinands and others training for ministry, provides a back-up for parishes which is far more effective than that offered by any 'official' Anglican organisation. It does have the drawback of all Evangelical 'para-church' bodies – it centres loyalties in the Society and not the Diocese but it can hardly be blamed for doing what Dioceses seem incapable of doing, namely providng attractive and biblical support facilities for local parishes. CYPECS has so effectively done that, that almost all its competitors seem to be tailing off in influence or looking distinctly outdated.

Leadership in the parish, across all traditions, has for centuries been in the hands of the incumbent and his churchwardens. Since the Enabling Act of 1919, some of this has been shared with Parochial Church Councils. Assistant curates have been given varying degrees of responsibility, usually in the area of youth work.

In the middle 1960s, Roy Henderson, then Vicar of St Luke's, Barton Hill, in the inner area of Bristol, set out to experiment with a 'lay eldership'.[98] He was encouraged by his bishop, Oliver Tomkins. Others began slowly to follow suit. In Fulham, Michael Botting set up such a scheme in the summer of 1972 which I inherited within a few weeks. By 1978, when I moved to Ealing, there was strong lay pressure for a similar scheme and it began in 1981.[99] By then, many parishes, mostly Evangelical, were experimenting with 'shared leadership'. From nearly fifteen years experience I can only speak gratefully of the enormous advantages of such team work. No two parishes seem to work in the same way but, if such schemes are prepared carefully, the benefits are out of all proportion to the problems incurred. Here again it has been Evangelicals who have led the way.

Another interesting development has been the growth of the use of 'parish administrators'. Mostly this has happened in urban parishes of middle to large sized congregations, able to afford the cost of setting up a parish office and employing on either a part- or full-time basis a lay man or woman to take over much of the daily 'business' of the church. Large city churches have for years been building up administrative teams but the extension to the ordinary church has only taken place in the late 1970s and 1980s. Much of the initiative has come from 'Administry', a small but campaigning organisation led by John Truscott, himself in past years an administrator in a city parish. Once again the impetus has come from Evangelicals. To someone like myself, who has been working with teams of elders, and an administrator, for almost a decade it is hard to remember what it was like in the days of the one-man-band vicar. Such an experience is increasingly influencing Evangelical clergy and ordinands. To them, the sharing of God-given gifts in parochial teams is what leadership in the local church is all about.

One benefit of such parochial team work has been the opportunity created for incumbents to spend more time in wider activities. Some with evangelistic gifts, like Michael Green and the late David Watson, are able to use them for the benefit of the Church at large. Others serve in the General Synod or on the various diocesan committees. Some write and broadcast. All are thus enabled to develop their gifts and use them to the full in Christ's service.

Very few parishes in England – Evangelicals included – can have much cause for complacency in the contemporary situation but where imagination and vitality go hand in hand with biblical teaching, shared leadership, prayer, fellowship and good young people's work, churches grow, or at worst, hold firm in the midst of the de-Christianising process which has undermined British society throughout this century and whose socially destructive influences seem to be reaching their zenith in the present decade.

It is in such a situation that many Evangelicals find themselves either cynically amused or positively angry when they hear of the occasional Bishop who makes public his intention of limiting, or undermining, the work of Anglican Evangelicals in his diocese. Such sentiments often seem to go hand-in-hand with a closed-mind bigotry (which is nowadays only rarely found among these same Evangelicals) and a pastoral ineptitude which seems incapable of welcoming spiritual growth and life unless it conforms to an image long since demonstrated to be impotent.

When such attitudes exist – and they do still exist today in some dioceses – it is hardly surprising that there are Evangelicals to be found in the Church of England who fight to maintain the historic patronage system, since it secures for them a continuing existence and a parochial continuity of churchmanship. Many – possibly most – Evangelicals support the reform of the system since (by their biblical principles) it is indefensible. But, and it is a big 'but', the antipathy of some of those who wield ecclesiastical power and patronage (occasionally with quite staggering blindness to their nepotistic appointments) is likely to do nothing but damage to the possibility of creating a more flexible structure for the benefit of the whole Church. It remains almost breathtaking when one realises that, despite an ordinand-production-line of about one-half of those being ordained, Anglican Evangelicals still find themselves virtually excluded from episcopal parochial appointments in many dioceses, and are openly told they are not wanted, in about 10% of the dioceses in the Church of England. Where they exist in such dioceses it is entirely due to the foresight of Charles Simeon and his friends, one hundred and fifty years ago, who purchased those advowsons and, thus, kept Evangelical religion alive within a handful of Church of England dioceses.

Those who, like myself, have not been conscious of being on the receiving end of such discrimination for the past twenty years, are nevertheless aware that such treatment is still openly thought desirable in a minority of dioceses. As J. Edwin Orr put it, of an earlier Evangelical movement, 'they enjoyed episcopal blessing as well as divine favour' in some dioceses 'but in others only the divine favour'.[100] It is hardly surprising, though doubtless regrettable, that Evangelical clergy so handled, regard their bishop as being of less than the *bene esse* of the Church!

Evangelistic impact

Partly because of their 'Evangelical' label and partly because of their concern for preaching for conversions, many assume that anything called 'Evangelism' will automatically attract all Evangelicals to its support. If that was ever true it certainly isn't today.

Josef Goebbels is as much an awful warning to Anglican Evangelicals as to many who distrust all mass oratory and its power to sweep crowds off their feet. While there are undoubtedly many who love mass evangelism and rejoice at the euphoria which often goes with it, there has in the past twenty-five years been a growing uneasiness about the methods and effects of some of the major campaigns and the use of what amounts to demagogy and mob-oratory at religious gatherings of other kinds. It isn't that most Evangelicals are opposed to mass-evangelism as such but rather that they are concerned to ask searching questions about whether the time, money, and effort involved could not be better spent at the local and personal level. Together with these questions are others about the inevitably 'Bible-belt' American culture which dominates most of the major campaigns and crusades. Such uneasiness is most frequently found among those clergy who work in the 'Urban Priority Areas' where the gulf between mass-Evangelism and the local culture is most marked. Many of them regard Evangelistic crusades as intrusions (and expensive ones) into the real work of ministry. It isn't that they aren't motivated by an Evangelistic fervour. It is the way in which they wish to express it that is so different. For a full generation the internal debate has gone on, punctuated regularly by another mass crusade. Should Billy Graham, or whoever, come again? He usually comes!

The existence of such a debate among those who are united in their support of Evangelism and want to reach a society adrift from its moorings with the gospel of Christ is surely a healthy sign? It demonstrates a movement's capacity for thoughtful self-examination when it can contain within its fellowship those who seem obsessed with mega-meetings alongside those who regard them as offering an evasion of the hard task of reaching the unchurched where they actually are.

What is missing from this debate, for the most part, is the personal acrimony which often mars such discussion when those outside the Evangelical 'tribe' join in. Almost all Evangelicals in England have a high regard for Billy Graham as a man and recognise that his Crusades since 1954 at Harringay Arena in London have done far more good than harm. Each one has produced a new wave of ordinands for the Church of England, quite apart from its considerable impact at a wider level. Few, however, would seriously argue that Graham has done more than scratch the surface of the problem and they wouldn't wish to blame him for that. He has after all, made the Christian faith newsworthy, which the mainstream churches have rarely been able to do, except when one of their leaders proclaims his inability to believe this, that, or the other article of the historic faith, except in some attenuated form.

Evangelism at the local level has also been a matter for internal controversy. Some parishes and clergy have proclaimed that so-and-so's new system (almost always from the American South) is what we have all been lacking. Others (like me), take one look at it and blench at the reduction of the gospel to slogan-eering and high-pressure door-to-door salesmanship. There is undoubtedly a real and proper place for the exposition of sin and guilt and the declaration that Christ alone forgives it but guilt-inducing techniques, with rapid amelioration assured, can often be a cruel deception and damaging to the soft-centred personality. No-one who values the name 'Evangelical' is likely to want to reduce the need for repentance and faith, based on the desire for forgiveness of sin but many who are unashamed to be Evangelicals find themselves embarrassed by the manipulative techniques adopted with gusto by some of their fellows. The thought of being swamped by satellite-TV pouring out high-pressure calls for souls to be saved ('put your hand on the set and say "I receive Christ"'); sicknesses to be cured on screen (or the victims to be rapidly pushed off-camera if the 'healing' doesn't 'take'); and tear-jerking pleas for 'dollars to sustain the Lord's wonder-working ministry through Brother X's TV station' is no more attractive to many Anglican Evangelicals than the vision of hours and hours of Don Cupitt's cerebral hang-ups being paraded for all to see!

It is perhaps the combination of a success-dominated culture, which majors on souls-dollars-and-bricks that has alienated more Anglican Evangelicals from Evangelism American-style than anything else. Sadly, our own attempts to do it at ground-level in a manner more appropriate to our own national culture have hardly succeeded and the failure encourages those who want to push the transatlantic package to do so even more strenuously. It is perhaps the saddest irony of English, and especially Anglican, Evangelicalism that its evident 'success' in recent decades has still not been extended into the area of effective and wide-spread Evangelism of the English nation. The only consolation to be had is that Anglican Evangelicals do it better than any other Anglicans here!

Social responsibility

I shall not easily forget the day in 1960 when I was firmly told by a senior Evangelical clergyman, with whom I was at the time working, that 'we don't want anything to do with Christian Aid – that sort of thing is nothing to do with the gospel, is it?' I don't say that such a view was held universally in Evangelical parishes in that era but it was certainly not uncommon. I was shocked and appalled. It wasn't that I had much social or political awareness myself. It was just that I couldn't believe that anyone could so easily divorce the Christian gospel from its practical outworking. I and my fellow curates set about converting our erring elder brother. What was almost equally disturbing was the ease with which we succeeded. The culprit, having dismissed the idea as outside the scope of the gospel, cheerfully capitulated, after three decades of indifference, within fifteen minutes of discussion!

Things are very different today. The elderly cleric mentioned above had grown up in the pre-war era when, as Randle Manwaring put it, Evangelicals had 'bought their citizenship at minimum cost, contributing little or nothing to political life or social well-being'. The turning point in this area was undoubtedly Keele in 1967. It is obvious to anyone reading the Keele Report that the four pages given to issues of social concern are full of well-meaning platitudes and little else. Nevertheless, they include the admission of 'shame that we have not thought sufficiently deeply or radically about the problems of our society'. The brief booklist appended – twenty-three titles – contained only nine by Evangelical writers and only two of those were treatments at a serious level.

Evangelicals in the eighteenth and nineteenth centuries had been in the forefront of social reform. Sometimes this was worked out in highly paternalistic ways but then that was the commonly accepted way of things at the time, however much E. P. Thompson may deplore the fact. By the late 1960s paternalism was not even a viable philosophy, even had it been desirable. The new pioneers were learning their lessons at both academic and street level and neither was a milieu calculated to look kindly on well-meaning do-gooders.

So what has happened in the past twenty years? Among Anglican Evangelicals certain names stand out. At Keele it was Sir Norman Anderson who paved the way and he followed this up with some excellent books.[101] Within two years, George Hoffman, one of the Eclectic, pre-Keele, 'agitators', was appointed to lead a newly-formed branch of the interdenominational Evangelical Alliance which was brilliantly christened 'TEAR Fund' from the initials of 'The Evangelical Alliance Relief Fund' and which has grown in less than twenty years to stand alongside Christian Aid as the two main non-Roman Catholic aid agencies. David Sheppard, after a dozen years in the East End of London, at Islington and Canning Town, was able to cross the river to Woolwich and exercise a widening ministry in which social and political elements would be publicised by his actions, his writing, and his general episcopal influence as, in due course, Bishop of Liverpool. He, and others drawn to him, greatly influenced the Report 'Faith in the City' and two fellow Evangelical clergy, John Gladwin, Secretary to the General Synod Board for Social Responsibility, since 1982, and Patrick Dearnley, Archbishop's Officer for Urban Priority Areas, have more than made their mark.

In the same period, 'Third Way', an interdenominational periodical, has offered a useful forum for debate for those involved in the social services and other related disciplines; while other Anglican Evangelicals have been deeply involved in politics, the voluntary services, education, broadcasting, race relations, sexual ethics, and the whole range of social and political questions which challenge contemporary society, both nationally and locally. Inevitably tensions have arisen when political allegiances have led into different packages of policies and philosophies but that was inevitable and it is probably a mark of maturing confidence that fellow Evangelicals can remain in Christian communion when their views differ so sharply. Peter Broadbent, Anglican chaplain at North London Polytechnic, and a Member of General Synod, is a Labour councillor in the London Borough of Islington, while Michael Alison, ex-Parliamentary Secretary to the Prime minister and a Conservative Member of Parliament is now Second Estates Commissioner at Millbank. Both are well known Anglican Evangelicals. To me, at least, that seems a healthy situation.

One sign that may cause surprise to those unaware of it has been the growing anxiety among the Anglican Evangelical missionary societies that they, the traditional outlet for world mission aspirations, are finding it harder and harder to sustain their financial commitments in the Third World, let alone increase their servicing ministry to the Anglican Provinces in Asia, Africa, and Latin America, due to the rapidly expanding work of TEAR Fund. Relationships remain excellent between these organisations but it is quite clear that those who have grown up in the 1970s and 1980s have been much more evidently moved by the visual evidence of human physical need than they have by the traditional Evangelical gospel of 'rescuing lost souls in darkness'. If anything the balance may have swung too far in the direction of alleviating physical and material deprivation at the expense of the good news of redemption. But, then, since the challenge of Liberation Theology even the idea of redemption has broadened. 'Kingdom' theology has also created further questions about the relationship of corporate and personal religious aspirations. No-one could say that present-day Anglican Evangelicals – certainly those who are averagely literate – are shut up in the old 'hot-gospel' ghettoes, immune to the agonies and conflicts of the world outside.

International contacts

As the world has contracted in the past twenty years so awareness of what is going on elsewhere has grown. Holidays abroad, sabbatical tours, international scholarships and personal friendships have all opened up vistas of how things are handled elsewhere and the way in which widely differing cultures respond to an Evangelical presentation of the Christian gospel. If I cite my own parish of Ealing, in West London, it may make the point. In the 1980s we have had among our congregation individuals from Australia, New Zealand, Hong Kong, Taiwan, South Vietnam, East Malaysia, Singapore, Iran, Iraq, Lebanon, Sudan, Kenya, Uganda, Tanzania, Zimbabwe, South Africa, Spain, France, Italy, Switzerland, Germany, Poland, Austria, Denmark, Sweden, Holland, Jamaica, Barbados, Guyana, Trinidad, Canada and the USA. We have contacts with Anglican Evangelicals working with the churches in Taiwan, Kenya, Tanzania, Argentina, and Ecuador. On my staff, for long or short periods, I have had men or women who have had experience (as nationals or expatriates) in New Zealand, East Malaysia, Kenya, Uganda, Tanzania, Holland and the USA. I have myself worked with Anglican congregations in France, Switzerland, Canada, Ghana, and five states across the USA. Add this huge collection together, and the cross-fertilization which results, and the one word which doesn't do it justice is 'parochialism'. It is a salutory experience to be verbally chastised from one's own pulpit by a go-getting Chinese brother-cleric for the way in which the English have squandered their Christian inheritance over the past hundred years.

Many of these international relationships have come about simply because of the ease of travel but others have developed more formally through missionary societies and the scholarship system organised by the Evangelical Fellowship in the Anglican Communion (EFAC). This scheme has brought one hundred, mostly Third World, Anglican Evangelical clergy to England where they have spent months, and often years, in theological colleges and supporting parishes. The mutual benefit usually far outweighs the disadvantages and can often lead to long-term links with churches and clergy from widely separate cultures.

At the highest levels, Evangelicals have played a significant, and sometimes major, role in Lambeth Conferences, on the Anglican Consultative Council, and through the Partners in Mission consultations across the world. So, too, they have held senior responsibility in the Partnership for World Mission. Names such as Simon Barrington-Ward, Alan Neech, John Stott, Festo Kivengere, Keith Sutton, Michael Harper and Jim Packer are known across the world.

Meanwhile, back at the ordinary parochial ranch, it is far more likely that an Evangelical congregation will be deeply committed to

Overseas mission than is the case with the average English parish church. One has only to see the amount of money, prayer support, and personal interest generated in an Evangelical parish to know that this is no idle, or triumphant boast. It's a fact.

Ecumenical concerns

Long before the modern ecumenical movement began (commonly attributed to the Edinburgh Conference of 1910) Anglican Evangelicals had been fellow-founders of the Evangelical Alliance in 1845, the Keswick Convention in the 1870s, and the Cambridge Inter-Collegiate Christian Union in 1877. Nevertheless, A. T. Houghton, one of the first of the modern Evangelical ecumenists, admitted frankly, in a paper given to the 1964 Nottingham Faith and Order conference, that 'historically the tendency among Evangelicals has been to divide rather than to unite'.[102] Their various inter-denominational activities were just that – they accepted the existence of denominations and offered fellowship to their fellow Evangelicals within these denominations. When they used slogans like 'All One in Christ Jesus' (the Keswick motto) they were content to be so for an annual week of spiritual companionship and then they returned home to denominational normality. The truth was, for late nineteenth and early twentieth century Evangelicals in the Church of England, that they neither cared much for debate about ecclesiology, ministry and sacraments nor did they have any desire, being a small minority, to find areas of disagreement with those outside the national Church with whom they enjoyed fellowship. In many districts it was the only real fellowship available to them since their brother-clergy scorned them.

It was the advent of the Anglican-Methodist unity proposals which sparked off the change of outlook which took place in the 1960s and 1970s. Although most Anglican Evangelicals were opposed to the scheme's Service of Reconciliation, many of them were faced, for the first time, with the question of what they actually did believe about Church, ministry and sacraments. 'All in each place' became the formula, following a book of that title, edited by J. I. Packer, which was published in 1965. I vividly remember my own 'conversion' to an ecumenical outlook since I actually preached myself out of one view ('spiritual unity') into another ('organic unity') during a sermon on Ephesians 4 in September 1964. It was Paul's metaphor of the 'body' which did it. How could one 'keep the unity of the Spirit in the one body' unless that most material of entities had some ecclesiological cash value? Within three months I was Secretary of Liverpool Council of Churches.

By 1967 the Keele Statement was spelling out in words of one syllable (or thereabouts) the conviction that the oneness of the Church 'finds its proper expression when all the Christians of a locality appear as a single visible fellowship, united in truth and holiness, displayed in love, service and worship (especially at the Lord's Supper), and active in evangelism . . . schisms, denominations and exclusive forms of fellowship are contrary to the biblical ideal'.[103] To add teeth to the new idealism, it continued, 'we cannot now rest content with a profession of being one in Christ with all believers if that profession becomes an excuse for refusing to seek local organic unity'.[104] Fine words!

In the intervening twenty years since Keele there is little doubt that Evangelicals in the Church of England have done much to improve their relationships with Christians of other traditions. At the local internal level they have far more to do with their fellow Anglicans than was the case. They frequently know, and have good relationships with, Roman Catholics as well as those in the historic Free Churches. The mood created by Vatican 2, on the one hand, and the Covenanting Proposals, on the other, helped this advance to take place and the general tenor of the ARCIC documents has been welcomed by the great majority of Anglican Evangelicals even if they have found themselves forced to oppose endorsements of too-comprehensive a nature in the General Synod. Even when finding themselves speaking and voting against specific Resolutions they have mostly made it clear that their opposition was not one of intransigence towards reunion discussions but only one of objection to what they see as a betrayal of biblical and patristic principles.

Rightly or wrongly, Evangelicals in the General Synod have been angered by regular attempts to tell 'both extremes' to stop being 'party-minded' on ecumenical matters. For fifteen years they have done all they could to support the Covenant Proposals and the ARCIC discussions while those of Anglo-Catholic persuasion appeared to play the 'party' game on issue after issue. When one has tried to honour the Keele principles it is not a little galling to see others behaving in quite a different way and then for you to be castigated by retiring Archbishops for one's alleged misbehaviour! It hardly encourages Evangelicals to be ecumenically minded, building up warm and much-valued relationships with Roman Catholics in which disagreements are seriously debated in a friendly way, while at the same time certain vocal and militant Anglo-Catholics openly deride

Christians in the Free and Independent churches, hardly recognising them as brothers and sisters in Christ. The hurt done to those in the mainline Free Churches must not be ignored.

The situation is, of course, different with regard to those who have an Independent polity. Inevitably, ecumenical attempts, from whatever quarter, were bound to founder in such a situation. Thus, the rise of the so-called 'House Churches' has not for the most part been welcomed by Anglican Evangelicals who, together with Evangelical congregations in the older Independent churches, have been regarded by many House Church leaders as fair game for blatant proselytising. The ethos of such groups has frequently been created by a mixture of 1960s anti-institutionalism, Christian pop-culture in the music field, sexual authoritarianism, fundamentalism, and various elements drawn from the Charismatic Movement. There is not a great deal of love lost between them and many of the Anglican Evangelical clergy who regard them as something of a cross between marauding bandits and totalitarian sects. Not all House Churches would merit such tough criticism and recently attempts have been made by the more moderate House Church leaders to re-open discussion with Evangelicals in the main denominations. It is frankly, hard to see that much can come of such cosmetic links unless the attacks on Anglican Evangelicals stop and the proselytism is abandoned.

Internal tensions

The Anglican Evangelical movement is, as has already been pointed out, a coalition rather than a party. Ten years ago there was much talk about an 'Evangelical identity crisis'[105] and today the tensions have, if anything, sharpened up even more. To get some idea of what is going on among Evangelicals within the Church of England it will probably be helpful if various groups are identified and their particular characteristics are delineated. Such groups are not, for the most part, to be thought of as mutually exclusive or at loggerheads with each other but it would be idle to pretend that their differences are not occasionally the cause for collision.

First, (though the order is not significant) there are *the Pietists*. Some of these are charismatic in theology, and some are not. To them, Evangelicalism is primarily a simple and convenient title for describing a particular form of spirituality. They are usually convinced that God is very directly concerned with their personal day by day experiences of life and they have no intellectual problem about expecting him to break in to even the most ordinary daily events. He will alter train and bus time-tables, almost to order. He will provide sunshine for church outings (even when farmers need rain). Pietists are great extempore pray-ers, though mostly for the people and issues on their daily doorstep. They read their Bibles enthusiastically and expect to find obscure passages from the Old Testament being actually fulfilled with an immediacy which sometimes takes non-Pietists' breath away. God is very real – he is behind every door, just as Satan is equally real – he is the immediate cause of every cough or stumble. Pietists are simple and trusting in their beliefs, love singing repetitive choruses and unrepentantly wallow in Zionistic language. Pietists instinctively distrust complex church structures like dioceses and synods. They sense compromise and faithlessness in the motivation of those who are involved in such activities. Pietists feel at home with Pietists and cannot really grasp why intellectuals and theologians make such heavy weather of everything. Pietists are high-octane believers, generous givers, spontaneous pray-ers, and some of them feel cheated unless they get a miracle-a-day. Pietists are high on love, fellowship, compassion, tears, and saving souls. Pietists are good, open-hearted people seeking and finding simple answers to complicated questions. There have always been plenty of Evangelical Pietists in every generation. They are not, in essence, unlike Catholic Pietists. There is, however, no such thing as a Liberal Pietist!

The second group are *the Parochials*. These have narrow, very narrow, horizons but will give themselves – heart, soul, and body – to their church and its immediate district. They care deeply for the spiritual and material well-being of those on their doorsteps and will give up everything – culture, leisure, family, and anything else you care to name – if a need arises in their immediate community. They know what is going on in that community and, if clergy, they will beat the ambulance to the hospital if someone is taken ill. Parochials regard all the more distant matters – ecumenism, church government, national politics, annual conferences, theological debate – as being unnecessary luxuries. They don't usually object to them and are glad that others (for some imponderable reason) are actually willing to get on and do them even though they *will* mess them up. Parochials do get angry about the mess caused by these other people and often vocally blame them but since they have neither the time, nor interest, they just have to close their eyes and get on with the job in hand, which is, as everyone knows, what life is really all about! Parochials are the people who have kept the Church of England afloat for twelve hundred years and while they aren't, by any means, all Evangelicals, no one can dispute that Evangelicals are really very good at being Parochials or at least they were until, as they see it, all this Team and Group Ministry nonsense started to rear its ugly head in the 1960s. As for that Sheffield business – well, the quicker Parochials are allowed to get on with their lawful duties, the better for the Church of England. That's their usual line!

Then there are *the Puritans*. There aren't as many as there were in the 1960s when it was bliss to get the Banner of Truth catalogue and begin to work one's way through those massive, dictionary-sized volumes of seventeenth century sermons and expositions. To know in detail what Calvin and Owen were thinking was, and still is, to them, the last word in Christian knowledge. Alas, alas, for the Arminian-oriented Anglican hierarchy whose theology was, in common with those wishy-washy Methodists, far from biblical. But to the faithful Baxter-inspired Reformed Pastor there remains the work of preaching and instructing, together with a close watch on the behaviour of the weaker brethren. And what a joy to gather annually at the feet of The Doctor. If only the Church of England had had more like him, but it was King Charles and his bishops who had taken the wrong road at the Restoration! Thank God for Whitefield and Toplady, for Warfield and Schaeffer. If only Packer would return from Canada . . . ! In the meantime keep up the Systematics, teach the children what TULIP means, hang on to the life-line still offered by the Independents, and God keep us from Charismatics.

We must not forget *the Protestants*. These are not what might justly be called 'Protesting Catholics' but 'Protestants' in the sense that they still look to the Edwardian Reformation (and to a lesser extent the Elizabethan Reformation) as the touchstone of all that Evangelicals should be striving to keep unsullied in the late twentieth century. Like all Evangelicals they hold to Scripture as supreme, justification as vital, and a non-sacerdotal doctrine of ministry as absolutely essential. But they go further. Most of them distrust modern liturgy, deeply dislike the Rite A communion service, look to preaching as the only valid means of communication of truth, fear sacramental language, and regard the Keele and Nottingham Congresses as largely regrettable events, hi-jacked by 'young activists of unconventional views'[106] who 'stage-managed' the resulting Reports. In recent years the Protestants have succeeded in capturing one of the Anglican Evangelical societies, with the expectation that they will, before long, control its patronage trust. They have sought – sometimes openly, sometimes not – to persuade the Evangelical community to eject well-tried members of General Synod (who are, in their view, compromisers) in favour of their own 'hard-line' candidates. Thus, in 1985, they secured a small, but aggressively vocal, group of lay men and women, pledged to oppose the ordination of women and all things Roman Catholic (especially the ARCIC proposals). The Protestants are numerically few but they function in ways not dissimilar to those adopted by the Socialist far left. Since there is always a certain amount of mileage in the Evangelical world to be secured by those who cry 'compromise, liberalism, and down with the Pope', the new Protestants may have a future. Whether they can recapture their lost ground (and they have lost huge tracts in the past thirty years) is very doubtful. Their one great advantage is that they are attacking what has for some years been the Evangelical 'establishment' and, since almost all the previous groups – Pietists, Parochials, and Puritans – are suspicious, on principle, of establishments, they may succeed in damaging that confidence which has been placed in the establishment. Time alone will tell. What certainly is difficult is for members of that Establishment to fight off what is sometimes character-assassination, spread by word of mouth, in shadowy corners! That rather melodramatic description happens to be a fact. It was a technique adopted (unsuccessfully) as early as 1975 when one prominent Protestant tried to canvass the unseating of two Evangelical members of the General Synod Standing Committee. On that occasion it rebounded quite decisively. Whether such methods can hope to succeed in 1990 remains to be seen. It will be evident from the above that the Protestants are a highly political group.

One ironical result of Protestant manoeuvring was the effective dismissal in 1983 of the Editorial Board of the theological magazine *Churchman* and the creation, in response, of *Anvil*. Large numbers of *Churchman* subscribers defected to *Anvil*, fearing what might happen to a periodical which some of them had read for decades. *Anvil*'s circulation is open to inspection whereas the *Churchman* figures do not now seem to be made public. They are thought to have declined dramatically.

All of which brings us to *the Powers-that-be*. Ensconced since Keele in most leadership positions within the Evangelical structures are a group of men and women, lay and clerical, numbering perhaps a hundred and fifty and chiefly in the forty to sixty-five age range; their influence has been decisive for two decades. They are the key figures in the Anglican Evangelical Assembly, (which has largely replaced the increasingly obsolescent Islington Conference, an annual gathering which for 150 years used to be the platform for Anglican Evangelicals), the Church of England Evangelical Council (the AEA's Standing Committee), the major Evangelical societies (with only one Protestant exception), the Evangelical theological colleges, the Evangelical Group in General Synod, and most of the various Evangelical publishing ventures. The same group provides the Evangelical bishops, Church Commissioners, Synod Standing Committee members, organisers of the National Evangelical Anglican Congresses and of the annual Senior Evangelical Anglican Clergy (i.e. over 40 year olds) conferences. From them, come most of those appointed to General Synod Boards, Councils and Commissions.

The *Powers-that-be* are far from clones but they do, without question, generally share a good deal of common ground. Few of them are hard-line Protestants. Few of them are strongly Charismatic. Few of them are Pietists, Parochials or Puritans though none of them would feel totally ill at ease with members of any of those groups. As one might expect, they cover the heart land of Evangelical belief and practice, while most of them are committed Anglicans and the majority of the clergy are men with considerable parish experience. They are rarely Fundamentalist, though almost all are conscientiously conservative in their biblical theology, easily able to affirm the new Basis of Faith (see pp.46–47 above). Politically they are wide ranging, incorporating Labour, Alliance, and Conservative convictions. Educationally, they are no longer dominated by Oxbridge and the major Public Schools. Socially, they are mostly middle class and a significant number have origins in the South East. If there is one conviction that unites them it is that the Anglican Evangelical movement ought to be mature enough to allow for a good deal of latitude of opinion while remaining grounded on the historical Evangelical theology. The relative ease with which the new theological Basis gained almost universal acceptance among them in 1986 indicates the common ground which they share.

Here, of course, it will be more than evident as to where my own sympathies lie. I have lived and moved within the structures of the Evangelical *Powers-that-be* for over twenty years. While my beliefs and my own spirituality are precious to me, I am not a Pietist. While the broad shape of my theology (as with most Anglican Evangelicals) has a Calvinist framework, I am not a Puritan. While I have spent twenty-six years as a Curate and Vicar in very varied parishes, I don't see myself as a Parochial. While I have never ducked the task of defending (in some very hostile places) many of the great Reformation (i.e. biblical) doctrines concerning Church, ministry, sacraments, and liturgy, I do not find that the label 'Protestant' sits easily on my shoulders.

And this is where the other aspects of my life come to the fore. I have enjoyed knowing a succession of Archbishops and working closely with one (in the Catholic tradition). I spent years in the ecumenical field. I tried to master the intricacies of the world of broadcasting for five years. I have enjoyed good friendships with Anglicans of every kind, from '60s Radicals to '80s Catholics. I have been beneficially influenced by men and women of almost every Christian tradition, in some way or other.

Why should I bother to mention these personal and autobiographical facts? Quite simply because I believe that many other Evangelicals in the Church of England have had comparable experiences and do not feel themselves to have been compromised thereby any more than I do. It is, as a result, mildly irritating to be told one is a hard-line Protestant by those in the Catholic group in General Synod and asked, patronisingly, why one 'stopped being an Evangelical' by the militant Protestant characters who have recently got themselves elected to Synod!

If I have one anxiety today about the Anglican Evangelical movement (and others share it) it would be 'will the numerical development ever bother to try to influence positively the Church of England?' When one has worked for three decades to bring what one believes to be the beneficial influences of a biblical Evangelicalism to bear upon the Church, at every level, it is sometimes discouraging to feel like a Commando, who having landed in Normandy on the night before D-Day, looks out to see the Army descending on the beaches in daylight, only to be told that they have decided to sing Choruses on the beach at Bognor because they don't think that you need their help and, anyway, it's much more satisfying!

It helps an Evangelical to have a sense of humour and it certainly isn't a universal gift.

4

Looking Ahead

As this book goes to Press, the 1988 Lambeth Conference is fast surging up over the horizon. Its themes have long since been known. Its letters from Chairmen and Vice Chairmen, asking for contributions from dioceses, have been widely disseminated. All over the world groups are at work, priming up their bishops' muskets with powder and shot. This, dear bishop, is what we think you should think and we hope that, before you come back home, what we think you should think will have helped others to think the same way. Only, we know it's not as simple as that, and you may well have to come back telling us what you think all those other bishops thought that we ought to think. Or not, as the case may be. And, in any event, since Lambeth Conference conclusions aren't mandatory, the best we can all hope for is a better set of bearings from that Compass Rose which has come to symbolise Lambeth Conferences. It may be hard to live with that depressing introduction to the 1978 Lambeth Report ('the resolutions have no legislative authority unless or until they have been accepted by the Synods or other governing bodies of the member Churches of the Anglican Communion, and then only in those member Churches')[107] but then that's the way it is with us Anglicans and we'd never hold together if anyone tried playing the Papal game.

That's as may be, but few Anglicans doubt the reality of the moral influence of Lambeth reports and resolutions. So perhaps one lower-deck Evangelical clergyman can express a few general words of unease at the way Lambeth Conferences are going?

First, and surely nobody can seriously question this, they are simply getting too big. Last time there were 407 on the 'voting strength' and this time it looks as if the number will be somewhere around 500. I recall attending the opening service at Canterbury Cathedral of the 1958 Lambeth Conference when the number of bishops present was 310 or thereabouts. Has the Anglican

Communion really grown at that rate in the last thirty years (if one discounts the Third World growth areas) or are Chiefs proliferating disproportionately to Injuns? (Incidentally, I do not 'discount Third World growth' for some toffee-nosed English reason. I thank God for it. But the huge growth in parts of Africa has not led to masses of African bishops at Lambeth.)

Which brings me to my second question. I have received nothing but hospitable warmth from North American Anglicans on three visits to the USA and Canada in the last decade. I do not wish to appear ungrateful or unfriendly if I say that their numbers at Lambeth grossly distort the numerical significance of their dioceses and provinces. Well over 100 from the USA and its related Latin American dioceses, plus over 30 more from Canada gives the 'North West' of America a speaking and voting strength of about a third of the Conference. The whole of Africa has fewer but how many Anglican Christians are there in Africa as compared with North America? Can we be sure that the resulting Report and resolutions will be free from 'cultural dominance' by one bloc, whose constituency is far smaller in aggregate than others who, for various reasons, are much less well represented in numerical terms? What about the 1998 conference being based on Provincial representation and closely related to the numerical membership of each one?

My last introductory comment concerns the consequences of the question 'what is a bishop?' For the past six years I have served on the General Synod's Dioceses Commission and we have been dogged throughout by that question. Is a Suffragan bishop really a bishop? And if he is, is he not entitled to be treated as a proper bishop at Lambeth conferences? Ought he, and his fellows, to be members, as of right? Clearly at present they are not and only the favoured few (whose favourites?) are invited. Surely, if the size of the Conference is getting out of hand, the proper solution is, as I have suggested, a Provincially structured conference, based on fair membership ratios, rather than the exclusion of so-called *real* bishops who are, in fact, less equal than others when it comes to Lambeth? The present method of choice puts an unfair burden on an embarrassed Archbishop of Canterbury who has, seemingly, to exclude most of the suffragans even though they have been validly consecrated as bishops in the Church of God.

Well, as I say, that's just my view and it has nothing to do with my being an Evangelical. But what are Evangelicals in the Church of England thinking when it comes to those 1988 Lambeth themes? No more than anyone else will they want merely to react after the

Conference is over. They too want to have their two-pennorth of input. So what is it likely to be?

What follows is, then, my own understanding of the way in which the Evangelical constituency has reacted, and goes on reacting, to the issues at stake. As will already have become clear, opinions will not be monolithic except perhaps in those areas of credal commitment in which to be an Evangelical is effectively to be an adherent to certain basic dogmatic convictions, grounded in Scripture and apostolic testimony. Almost by definition to be an Evangelical (or a Catholic for that matter) means that 'fully God and fully man' is not a matter for Anglican debate!

Mission and ministry

The natural first reaction which many will have to the questions posed by Bishops Festo Kivengere (who has sadly had to stand down from the chairmanship of the group) and David Sheppard, both men nurtured in the Evangelical tradition, is to ask, 'what happened to the question Why?'

The nine questions proposed are all excellent and will repay thoughtful study but none of them attempts any kind of analysis (the 'why' question) of what it is which, negatively, hinders effective Christian mission in some parts of the world and what, positively, leads to real impact being made elsewhere. 'Why is, or was, the Church so effective at this or that point in history in this or that place?' Such a question naturally leads on to ask whether there are any indispensible elements in the nature of the gospel as it was, or needs to be, proclaimed in concept, word or action? Unless these analytical questions are tackled at the foundational level this whole section of the Conference will spend all its time on the 'technology' questions, 'How', and 'What'?

Let us pursue this further. Nearly forty years ago Donald McGavran in his seminal book, *Bridges of God*,[108] argued from his Indian experience that 'missionary' work was doomed to failure in strongly tribal-type communities unless the whole group agreed to change its allegiance from its old gods to the Living God. This method of mission, he argued, had a long history. It was, broadly, the way in which Western Europe had been 'Christianised' in the Dark Ages. Not until post-Renaissance man, with his consciousness of his individualism, came on the scene did the Church, or certain parts of it, set about the task of individual evangelism with personal conversion becoming the goal.

Has this lesson been applied in those parts of the Third World which are still strongly tribal and paternalistic? Was it found to be effective or not? Has it been in anyway instrumental in the Evangelisation of those parts of Asia, Africa, and Latin America which have moved into the Christian churches since the Second World War? I do not know the answer. McGavran's thesis may have proved mistaken in its application. But has it been evaluated by the Anglican Communion?

Just suppose that McGavran was right and that the evidence is available to demonstrate the fact. Would that be the key to all world mission? Would that support the teaching of ethnic mission, leading to ethnic churches, which has been persuasively argued by the Californian Church Growth pundits in recent years. Or would it not be open to argument that ethnic churches perfectly fit California, keeping those of varying colours, languages, and cultures comfortably apart and all in the name of 'effective Church Growth'? How convenient if the rich and poor can be cheerfully segregated in the name of Christian mission? How very satisfying if parts of Africa can be kept hermetically sealed from the surrounding tribes who can be encouraged to be 'their sort' of Christian while 'we' stay ours. How much more effective if 'our' bishop comes from 'our' tribe and not from theirs? For 'our tribe', read 'Sloanes' in Kensington, 'Ivy Leagues' in New England, and 'Scouse' in Merseyside. What are the implications if, in Britain, it seems more effective to have 'black churches' rather than multi-racial ones. Where does Paul's clarion-call to the Ephesians stand if it be more effective to keep Jew and Gentile apart in the name of Evangelistic efficiency? And, more difficult still, what ought we to do, if it proves to be evidently effective in Evangelistic terms to do just that? What are the social and theological limits to the price which can be paid in the name 'successful mission?'

Another preliminary question would occur to most of those in the Evangelical tradition: why bother to indulge in all that goes by the name of mission unless you have agreed about its necessity and goal? One of the most distinctive elements in the Church of the 60s (and the consequences are still with us, at least in Europe and parts of North America) was the loudly-trumpeted proclamation by the Radicals that 'the world writes the agenda' for the churches whose task, as mission, is to trot along behind, counter-signing all that we find since, of course, Christ got there long before we did. Is it a caricature to suggest that such a theology means no more than telling a Buddhist that, if he only had eyes to see, he would realise that he was actually a crypto-Christian! That kind of soteriological universalism, slightly deodorised perhaps, still seems to be widely inherent in much Anglican church life today. Yet, to be honest, what is the need for proclaiming salvation, uniquely to be found in Jesus Christ, if the hearer is already covered by a universal and eternal life assurance policy or if his political, social, sexual and cultural ethics are similarly welcomed by a God whose capacity for moral and religious compromise is prodigious and unlimited?

Mission, as a concept, has greatly (and rightly) widened in its meaning in the past two decades. It is no longer taken to be merely a synonym for personal Evangelism. In this respect the Keele Statement in 1967 was more comprehensive than the succession of bitty references in the Nottingham Report of 1977. Keele defined Mission as 'the activity by which God works to restore the World to harmony with himself'. It is not, it went on, 'a technique by which the Church expands itself' since 'God's purpose is to make men new through the gospel, and through their transformed lives to bring all aspects of human life under the Lordship of Christ'. We, as Christians, are called to 'share in God's work of mission by being present among non-Christians to live and speak for Christ, and in his name to promote justice and meet human need in all its forms'. Since 'Evangelism and compassionate service belong together in the mission of God' this 'is the work of the whole people of God'.[109]

Here, surely, is where the Lambeth group on Mission and Ministry should start. Here is an excellent and wide-ranging definition of Mission. Since it also includes references to a God who 'is always active in saving love and in judgment within his rebellious world', it can go on to speak of Christ 'through whom men alone are redeemed', and yet not hesitate to affirm the biblical and traditional Christian conviction that 'a persistent and deliberate rejection of Jesus Christ condemns men to hell'.[110]

Such a starting point for the Lambeth group's discussions would set them on firm ground. Mission would be a necessity with both positive and negative goals. It would offer the world a clear-cut challenge from a loving and holy God. It would assure Christians that their task was not optional but essential. If the Lambeth fathers could call the Church to such a task, all the questions about 'how' and 'what' would fall more easily into place. They would be no less important as questions but they would all hold together as parts of one agreed task and defined target.

I want to take up only one and it is the first. 'What is the nature of Christian proclamation in a world where all authorities are questioned?' I want to question that statement. It is not evident to me that 'all authorities are questioned'. Our world is full of incompetent and unreliable authorities whose very word is law. Virtually every political leader, every top sportsman, every pop star, every odd-ball guru, every media personality, all of these, and others, exercise great influence over those who rely on their judgment (even in areas where they appear to know almost nothing!). The degree of popular gullibility is quite frightening. It would surely be a much better world if some of these so-called 'authorities' were questioned a great deal more?

However, these and similar 'authorities' have, over the past half-century, frequently conveyed the impression that, while none (or few) of them would deny the existence of God, the fact is not of much consequence when it comes to working out what they believe and how they behave. The result is that while the number of professing atheists in the so-called 'Free World' is very small, the number of 'committed Christians' in Europe and North America is, especially in the former, a minority.

How then do we 'proclaim' Christian truth to a very confused people? Not, in all probability (if we are to be believed by the bulk of a disaffected population) by 'shouting even louder'. That works no better in such a situation than it does across language barriers. So what is the answer?

Not, I suggest, simply by being moral, upright and respectable citizens. Gordon Harman, an Anglican rector I once worked with trenchantly posed the question, 'who gets the glory?' Certainly, as far as the English are concerned, you are respected if you live an upright life but *you* are the one who gets whatever credit is going – none of it goes to Christ. So, there must be at least some pointing to him as the motivator of a distinctly Christian life-style. To act in a way that all believe to be an outstanding example of a different quality of life – that requires some interpretation. In this sense, 'actions speak louder than words' is a false aphorism. The truth is that 'actions speak loudest with words'. Neither carries conviction, in Christian terms, without the other.

Hand in hand with that needs to go the slow explanatory building up of confidence in the good news of an incarnate God. Neither Bible, nor Church, is likely to win allegiance if the life-style does not challenge the continuous compromise of most people's daily life. But, when it does, the authority of Christ and the apostolic testimony becomes powerfully persuasive. A Church that is made up of people who lovingly live and teach the reality of a Saviour and Lord rarely has much problem about its authority – people are amazed by it. It changes lives and makes a Christian community – the local church – a lighthouse for the gospel. Couple that up with intelligent, thoughtful, and genuinely confident apologetics and people start to sit up and take notice! The authority governing such a community, its lifestyle and its beliefs will certainly be open to question but the questions will be urgent not hostile. As a self-confessed middle-aged Existentialist said to me, just prior to his Confirmation recently, 'my philosophy for the past twenty years has been utterly selfish and it has proved quite incapable of coping with life's harshness – it has nothing to say in the face of tragedy, suffering, and death. It was exciting when I was twenty. It is literally hopeless as you get older'. He drank in the good news of Jesus Christ. It all made sense, rational sense.

Perhaps the Church in the Western democracies has made the profound mistake of putting its most hesitant spokesmen in the forefront of the action. In the dioceses, the universities, in the media, in the cathedrals, it is those who give the impression that the unbelieving world is probably right, who get the top billing. What other organisation would do such an extraordinary thing? Well, the damage has been done. The undermining voice of liberal Christianity has had its chance and we are all facing the consequences of its failure. Perhaps Lambeth should pin its hopes for Mission on a God who acts, who speaks, and whose power transforms individuals and communities when it is proclaimed and demonstrated with love, trust, and confident faith. Heaven knows, it's time the Anglican Church pulled its finger out and let God get in on the action!

Dogmatic and pastoral concerns

Reading the previous paragraph you might well be forgiven for thinking that it fits perfectly into Archbishop Keith Rayner and Bishop James Yashiro's category of those 'demanding a more forceful re-affirmation of our traditional doctrinal formularies'. You would, of course, be right – up to a point. It has always been a mark of the Evangelical that he doesn't lightly modify, or welcome modification, of the faith once delivered to the saints. He sees a coherence of doctrine running through the Scriptures and he finds its fulfilment in the incarnate life, death, resurrection, and ascension of Jesus Christ and in the apostolic interpretation of that sequence of events. He welcomes, if he is an Anglican, the development of those teachings in such ways as remain consistent with them. Where he

parts company with other Christians is at the points historically and theologically when they – whether as individuals or even as Ecumenical Councils – so interpret the apostolic testimony (that unique deposit of the Faith) as to distort it, to diminish it, to augment it, or even to negate it. These, if you like, are his quartet of verbs which shape a kind of Chalcedonian formula about his understanding of the divine revelation of truth.

It needs to be stressed that, both for Evangelicals and for Roman Catholics, Holy Scripture is 'the ultimate, permanent and normative reference of the revelation of God'.[111] Despite the inevitable questions about interpretation which rightly concern all Christians, that unique quality about the Bible is, to use the words of the General Synod's House of Bishops, that it is 'paramount, for all Christians'. It is 'the inspired record and interpretation of God's love' and 'the Scriptures, therefore, both Old and New, must always have a controlling authority ... under which we need to place ourselves continually'.[112]

Historically, and in its formal statements, there can be no doubt where the Church of England stands. It stands firm on the intrinsic authority of an inspired record, 'the apostolic faith ... uniquely revealed in the Holy Scriptures'.[113]

The issues then, at least to all those who take seriously the understanding expressed by the Roman Catholic Church, by the Anglican churches, and by Evangelicals (whether Anglican or not) are not to do with the uniqueness of the inspired revelation. It is the Word of God (recognised to be so both theologically and liturgically) and for both the latter groups it 'must always have a controlling authority'. For Roman Catholics its authority is not a 'controlling' one since that is 'entrusted to the living, teaching office of the Church alone'.[114]

Where the problems arise, certainly in the Church of England, are the limits, or otherwise, which are consistent with the canonical requirement 'to proclaim afresh' this faith, 'in each generation'.[115] No one questions the necessity of such a task. The most conservative of Anglican Evangelicals would gladly endorse it. Even those who most distrust what they think is wrapped up in the word 'hermeneutics' all recognise that only the most sterile of fundamentalisms can treat the Bible as capable of being ripped absolutely out of its ancient context and applied with total literalism and in its most absolutist sense to the world of the late 1980s. In the Report of their seven-year dialogue on mission, the Roman Catholic and Evangelical participants (only a few of whom were Anglicans) make the point effectively. Their comments are worth quoting at some length since they set out interpretative criteria which can only be of service to the Lambeth fathers.

'What', they ask first, 'did the authors intend to say? What did they intend us to understand. For this is the "literal" sense of Scripture, and the search for it is one of the most ancient principles which the Church affirmed. We must never divorce a text from its biblical or cultural context, but rather think ourselves back into the situation in which the Word was first spoken and heard.

To concentrate entirely on the ancient text, however, would lead us into an unpractical antiquarianism. We have to go beyond the original meaning to the contemporary message. Indeed, there is an urgent need for the Church to apply the teaching of Scripture creatively to the complex questions of today... in this dialectic between the old and the new, we often become conscious of a clash of cultures, which calls for great spiritual sensitivity. On the one hand, we must be aware of the ancient cultural terms in which God spoke his word, so that we may discern between his eternal truth and its transient setting. On the other, we must be aware of the modern cultures and world views which condition us, some of whose values make us blind and deaf to what God wants to say to us'.[116]

So far, so good. Few will disagree with that. But what about the pre-suppositions which we bring to our study? To anyone who has read some of the reductionist works of radical academics in the past twenty years the next section may ring bells of instant recognition.

'What we must seek to ensure', they add, 'is that our pre-suppositions are Christian rather than secular. Some of the pre-suppositions of secular philosophy which have vitiated the critical study of the Bible are (a) evolutionary – that religion developed from below instead of being revealed from above – (b) anti-supernatural – that miracles cannot happen and that therefore the biblical miracles are legendary – and (c) demythologizing – that the thought world in which the biblical message was given is entirely incompatible with the modern age and must be discarded'.

Others, who have looked to the World Council of Churches for their bed-time reading, may smile at the final comment. 'Sociological pre-suppositions', they conclude, 'are equally dangerous, as when we read into Scripture the particular economic system we favour, whether capitalist or communist, or any other'.[117]

I have included this extended passage because it appears to me to make the essential point about the biblical commentator's pre-suppositions. Recent controversy about the nature of the Virgin Conception and the Empty Tomb demonstrates only too well the pre-suppositions of those who question the traditional, biblical and patristic meaning of those events. It would seem that if modern secular man finds such material happenings hard to swallow, some would let such pre-suppositions persuade them to jettison the alleged events or replace them with Gnostic alternatives. Can such 'fresh proclamation of the faith' be permitted as authentic? 'Not so', say both the Houses of Clergy and Laity of the Church of England's General Synod. 'Not officially', says the Synod's House of Bishops, trying rather too obviously to have its cake and satisfy the more exotic tastes of a handful of its members.

The one really unhelpful response to all this is to reduce it all to slogans, anti-slogans and smear-words. In a recent article in *The Independent* newspaper, Kenneth Leech maintained in his usual strident way that 'fundamentalism is the enemy of all true spiritual theology. 'It is,' he continued, 'a form of illness, a pathological growth upon religion'.[118] What he, and many others like him, never do is to define the word when they use it. For two generations 'Fundamentalist' has been a choice 'dirty-word' to be flung about promiscuously at all who hold to any positive view of the Bible's authority. On this reckoning, all the Church of England's formal statements about the Bible are fundamentalist. I well recall how in the early 1960s, I was being interviewed by a well-known liberal clergyman for an overseas post. 'Are you a Fundamentalist?' he enquired. I asked him to define it before I replied. That alone terminated the conversation after seven minutes. Never mind that I, like most Anglican Evangelicals, firmly reject the title as a self-description. To ask for a definition was to stand condemned. Today the word is rapidly coming to mean 'anyone who treats his sacred books seriously'. Thus today it is a smear-word for describing Christians and Muslims alike. It is particularly ironical that some of those who use the word most aggressively seem to Evangelicals to be themselves suffering from a peculiar pathological neurosis which maintains dogmatically that all who hold firmly to Scripture's inherent inspiration and authority must be wrong since everyone knows that absolutist dogmatic convictions are 'pathological'. Unless of course, they happen to be your dogmatic convictions in which case they are self-evidently true. Something similar is happening to the Johannine language of 'new birth'. If Lambeth 1988 could fly a battle-flag in favour of the need to define terms – especially terms with a long history of mis-use – it would certainly help the ecumenical task of understanding and reconciliation in the sphere of theology and dogmatics. As to the matter of the Divine inspiration of the Bible, it is worth remembering that William Temple, in his Gifford Lectures, described the view (held by Evangelicals) as being 'that which has been traditional in Christendom throughout the greater part of Christian history'.[119] The danger of 'falling off the end of the theological world' is surely greater for those who proffer novel solutions than for those whose beliefs have a direct lineal and theological connection with the apostolic doctrines. To be part of a Church which allows and encourages some element of exploratory work 'on the frontiers' of theology may well be a sign of maturity. One can hardly be so encouraged when those holding the heart and core of the apostolic *kerygma* and *didache*, whose tradition is fast becoming, in England, the largest segment of Anglican life, can still be dismissed, with undefined sloganeering, as being a diabolical influence!

What then, in brief, are the consequences of a strong doctrine of Scripture (which needs in no sense to be the same as the real 'fundamentalism' of strict literalism, in which the Bible is no more than a vacuum-packed compendium of texts)? Surely, first, the recognition that while there are different emphases in Scripture there is a single coherent theme which integrates those writings, namely that God has made a Covenant with a People, whom he has called to be uniquely his and that this People come from the whole breadth of humanity. They are those who acknowledge Christ to be God's unique incarnation in whom alone is God's saving purpose fulfilled and through whose Spirit redemptive life begins, continues, and finds its completion in an ultimate integration when all that is caught up in God's eternal plan finds its place.

One corollary of this is that however much the animating work of the Spirit sweeps across all humanity it is only when the focus sharpens on to Christ's incarnate life, death, and resurrection that the means of salvation become clear. There, and there alone, do all humanity's self-justificatory, merit-based, systems of religion and morality come face to face with a loving God who judges all that seeks to reach him by its own inherent morality and religiosity and offers in its place free, un-merited grace for all who will look to Christ, and Christ alone, as the divinely-provided means of reconciliation, available for all humanity. That understanding of 'good news' is axiomatic to all who take the coherence of the Bible seriously and it colours all their responses to the world's ideologies and religions. Christianity is, thus, not *one* of the world's religions to be set in relation to all the others and evaluated accordingly but, rather, God's unique way, offered freely, to all of every culture, race, religion and class who seek to be restored to fellowship with their maker. While the Christian Church may rightly welcome all that turns men's thoughts to a creator and all that works for peace and justice, from whatever source, it cannot, if it be true to its Redeemer's revelation of himself and his purpose, demote him from his unique, his 'once-for-all', ministry on behalf of all mankind.

This understanding of God's eternal purposes uniquely focussed in the Semitic Asian, Jesus of Nazareth, fully God yet fully man, calls forth (or ought to call forth) a solidarity on the part of his followers with the whole of sinful humanity. Thus a *de haut en bas* attitude to people of other religions and ideologies is utterly inappropriate. It may well be important, at some point, to offer a critique of a philosophy which, say, denies that there is any reality since all is illusory or which argues that there is little objective meaning to good-and-evil since all forces are in balance. These ideas, like others down the centuries, may need questioning in the name of a God who calls matter 'good' and who permits, in temporal terms, 'evil' to exist. Truth, in Christian understanding, pre-supposes that there is falsehood and error and that it needs exposing. All this is a corollary of biblical revelation. But, by the same terms, a second corollary is the avoidance (*à la* Publican and Pharisee) of any personal claim to self-righteousness, or even institutional self-righteousness claimed for the Church. Evangelism is one beggar telling another beggar where to find bread. Yet, though both are consciously beggars, there *is* bread and only one has found it. There is no love demonstrated by the beggar who jealously hoards his bread on the grounds that his fellow-beggar is better off with what he has (or hasn't) got. It is worth recalling that the beggar illustration came from an Asian not a White Westerner!

Ecumenical relations

'Of all the items... on church agendas,' wrote Colin Buchanan in 1977, 'unity is the one which consistently wins top prize for the highest ratio of input of paper to output of action. My shelves', he added, 'measure the stuff by the yard; I have contributed my own share to it; much of it is unreadable; virtually all of it is dated; most Christians seem bored to tears with it; and still it comes . . . there is no close season'.[120] Buchanan was voicing a weariness which hangs like a pall over many Christians, Evangelicals among them. To call, as many of us did in 1964, for 'Unity by Easter 1980' was a splendid, youthful, rush of ecumenical blood to the head but in the intervening years the blood seems to have congealed in one hardened artery after another. It was, after all, heart-warming for a young Anglican Evangelical, whose local Roman Catholic parish priest would not, in 1961, even speak to him in the street, to hear stirring tales of Vatican Two or to sit alongside Michael Green in Kings College, London, as two excited young curates listened to Hans Kung lecturing in terms which had seemed totally unthinkable even five years earlier. 'He sounds just like Luther', we said to each other in the state of glazed, but delighted, shock with which we afterwards emerged into the Strand.

Times have certainly changed. The most that can today be realistically hoped for in the direction of the English Free Churches is that polite courtesy which exists between would-be spouses, one of whom has jilted the other in answer to the crucial question, 'wilt thou have this woman to thy wedded wife?'. Even worse when the spouse-to-be has led two ladies up the garden path inside fifteen years! So, while personal local relationships may, in places, flourish and hopes be raised for 'ecumenical projects' of a lawful nature, there is little to excite the blood in that direction and a good deal of very understandable politely bored chit-chat over the garden wall on that side of the Anglican back garden. Enthusiasts may rabbit on about taking down the fence and jointly tending both lawn and herbaceous borders but most of us know that, sadly, nothing drastic is going to happen before the end of the twentieth century. It costs very little to make appreciative noises about World Council of Churches reports on 'Baptism, Eucharist and Ministry' and even to pick out little plums from it for admiring comment. That's no more than making clucking noises over photographs of next-door's baby. 'Isn't he sweet?' we say and get on with minding our own family's business. Evangelicals are no different from anyone else when it comes to polite small talk, and the occasional picnic, with the neighbours on that side of the back fence.

It's a bit different with the people in the big, detached, house on the other side, They have, it's true, stopped ignoring us and nowadays they have us on their guest list. We often talk about religion and politics but since they know exactly where they stand

and we sound rather like the SDP on a bad day it's not beyond the bounds of possibility that they might buy us out for rather less than we're worth if we don't keep out eyes skinned. They are, after all, experts in the game of smiling sweetly while the bailiffs go in!

That, not entirely far-fetched, piece of domestic imagery gives something of the flavour currently existing among Anglican Evangelicals towards the Roman Catholic Church. Changes, tremendous and positive, there have undoubtedly been in the last quarter-century. The Anglican Roman Catholic International Commission (ARCIC) reports have been, for the most part, creative and hopeful documents and to most Evangelicals in the Church of England reveal possibilities for future dialogue which must clearly continue. Only the smallest minority of hard-line Protestants would actively want to stop the process.

Yet all is not entirely well. Those most urgently wanting a decisive change in relations between the Anglican and Roman Catholics are perhaps rather too obviously using the whip as if they only had a furlong to go when reality suggests that we are only just crossing the water-jump, with all of the second circuit to go, Beechers, the Canal Turn and all those lesser fences still before us.

Let me illustrate this from the key debates in November 1986 in which the General Synod was asked to make its response to the three Statements on Eucharist, Ministry and Authority.[121] The motions dealing with the first two used the phrase that the Statements and their Elucidation were 'consonant in substance with the faith of the Church of England'. As regards the Eucharist, it has been clear for years that the essential questions concerning Presence and Oblation were becoming more evidently understood on all sides and even those of us who voted against in Synod were in many cases only saying that 'consonance in substance' was rather too strong a phrase and that 'convergence' would have been a more accurate description. In the event, while the House of Bishops voted (33–0) in favour, the vote in the House of Clergy (189–27) and the House of Laity (141–65) indicated that the matter was not yet unanimous or, in the case of the Laity, anywhere near to being so. Having said that, the vote on the Eucharist shows a very substantial support.

From that point onwards things get more and more difficult. The General Synod vote on the Ministry Statement followed hot-foot after a debate on 'The Priesthood of the Ordained Ministry' in which, broadly speaking, the doctrine of ministry presented in the ARCIC Report was subjected to a sustained and hostile critique. In the end, the Faith and Order Advisory Group's report on the Priesthood was virtually disembowelled, only just surviving (224 votes to 207) an amendment to declare its concluding section as being inconsistent with the early biblical section.[122] It is not unfair to say that the doctrine of Priesthood in the FOAG report came close to that in the ARCIC Statement and led to virtually one hundred members of Synod voting against the ARCIC motion which declared it 'consonant in substance with the faith of the Church of England' thus providing 'a firm basis upon which to move towards the reconciliation of the ministries of our two communions'.

The two debates (FOAG and ARCIC) demonstrated unmistakably that Anglican Evangelicals (with, it must be admitted, some surprising exceptions) do not find the ARCIC and FOAG doctrines of ministerial priesthood either biblical or consonant with the Church of England's faith. It is hard to see any way in which the necessary two-thirds majorities can possibly be obtained in future years (in a growingly Evangelical Church of England). Ministerial priesthood, except in its Anglican Reformation sense (which is nothing like the meaning foisted upon it by FOAG and ARCIC), is quite evidently a doctrine unknown to the New Testament and, indeed, in their sense, to the pre-Nicene Church's doctrine of the presbyterate.[123]

As to ARCIC on Authority, the uneasiness about what is likely to be involved spreads far wider than the Anglican Evangelical constituency. In the Synod Vote, 42% of the House of Laity could not accept that there was even 'sufficient convergence' between the two Communions 'to explore further' the issues.

The idea that these strongly attested hesitations, largely from among the Evangelicals, are no more than puppet-like manifestations of the old 'no popery' syndrome, is miles wide of the target. The desire to explore issues of theology and ecclesiology between Evangelicals and Roman Catholics is here to stay, as evidenced by the seven-year discussions cited on various occasions in this book. An excellent and eirenic example of an attempt to spell out the major problems which remain between Roman Catholic and Protestant (using the word non-polemically) Churches has been recently provided by Peter Toon.[124]

The issues are, of course, wider than the ARCIC subjects and cover the actual realities of popular devotion as well as the sophistication of ARCIC-level discussion. The question of Mary's role in the life of the Church, the popular understanding of salvation and piety, the place of women in ministry and the possibility of lay presidency at the eucharist are all areas in which widely differing convictions and practices exist, or soon might. To these must be added the ongoing disputes about sexual practices, divorce, mixed-marriages, abortion and genetic engineering.

To say then that Anglican Evangelicals and Roman Catholics have significantly changed their traditional views about each other is to speak the truth. But to say that all is now only a matter of tidied-up semantics and putting right a few embarassing historical misunderstandings is to talk the language of cloud cuckooland. And, what is worse, such disingenuous attitudes set back the cause of real dialogue. At the end of the day, effective dialogue only takes place when those who know where they differ and why, meet to talk, study and pray together. On those occasions the fewer of the people who think of themselves as 'moderates' there are present, the better it is for everyone. The so-called moderates hardly ever understand the real issues. Plenty of Roman Catholics and Anglican Evangelicals understand that fact only too well. The others simply function like loose horses at the Grand National – they get in the way of the real competitors! That may sound unflattering and even impertinent but almost all of those who stand firmly within the two different dogmatic traditions know that it is a plain fact!

Christianity and the social order

Since Keele, the matters raised in this field have become areas in which it is quite impossible to discover a common mind among Anglican Evangelicals. There is no agreed policy concerning systems of government; international relations; economic theories; war; nuclear weapons; justice; the appropriate methods of, and limits to, punishment; education; medical politics and ethics. On and on go the arguments.

The Nottingham Congress of 1977 demonstrated this with absolute clarity. A document on 'Power in our Democracy' was prepared by one of the group but when the final report was published it was complemented, or contradicted, by a second statement set in juxtaposition.[125] They broadly represented the views of political Left and Right. Both are equally evident among Evangelicals.

Thus the only fair advice which an Evangelical can present to the Lambeth fathers on this huge area is to say 'we are no more united than you and quite possibly a great deal less so'. We have our men and women of both Left and Right. Both think their way is the biblical and Christian one. Yet, at the end of it all, while we seek to root our convictions in Scripture, our conclusions look remarkably like party manifestoes at election time.

We are perhaps more united in seeking to strengthen the family, especially in its fast-disintegrating position in Western society. Most of us hope that the Lambeth fathers will place their weight behind the concept of the family, however locally expressed, as the fundamental God-given building block of human society even if superseded in the Kingdom of God by the Church as the family among whom 'water is thicker than blood'.

Most Evangelicals look to Lambeth also to speak plainly and compassionately about the incompatibility of homosexual genital relations with the Christian faith and especially with its public ministry. The recent advent of AIDS has, rightly, caused many Christians to want to speak words of sensitive kindness to those who have contracted the disease, especially through non-sexual means, but there can be no drawing back from the need to declare the historic and biblical tradition, without compromise, that while a homosexual orientation may, and often is not, a matter of individual volition the expression, in genital contacts, is, and in the Christian tradition has virtually universally been, a practice held to be inconsistent with the pursuit of holy living.[126] Let the Lambeth fathers declare this, as, hopefully, they will also declare fornication and adultery to be unacceptable behaviour within the Christian community. For the past twenty years the Anglican Church's spokesmen's failure to speak unequivocally about these things, however unpopular that voice may be, has been a contributing factor to the sexual promiscuity which now threatens to become the behavioural norm in many of the nations where the Anglican Church is a significant presence. To proclaim a message of forgiveness for sin, including sexual sin, is what the gospel is about, but for there to be meaningful forgiveness there must be a recognition of what sin is, whether it be injustice, greed, corruption or the misuse of God's gift of human sexuality.

Lambeth 1988 has set its hand to huge tasks. In reality, and considering the time available, the tasks chosen may well turn out to be far beyond the bishops' capacity. God preserve them from strings of platitudes. The risk of making dozens of common-place, pious noises is evident enough to anyone who has read the 1978 Lambeth Report.

Anglican Evangelicals will be praying for the 1988 Conference, that it may avoid these and similar pitfalls as it seeks to speak a prophetic word to our Communion and, beyond it, in the coming year.

5

Conclusion:
Is the Carnival Over?

There seems to be a rumour going around that the future lies with the Evangelicals. They are the ones who, in the jargon, have the ball at their feet. This book's title, as originally proposed to me, was to have been 'Evangelicals on the March'. I played hard to get. 'On the Move', I can live with. 'On the March' carries all those triumphalist vibes that are beloved of our transatlantic cousins. No way, said I.

It isn't that I don't want to see the Evangelical influence growing in the Church of England and out into the wider Anglican Communion. Of course I do. Not for some 'party' reason but simply because I believe that what Anglican Evangelicals stand for is of quite crucial significance to the world-wide Church.

Sixty years ago a great, if eccentric, old Evangelical and very Protestant clergyman called Daniel Bartlett was being amicably chided by the then Archbishop of Canterbury. 'What does it feel like, Bartlett,' smiled the Great Dignitary, 'out there, right out there, on the extreme end?' 'No, Your Grace,' retorted Bartlett, flashing his impish, mouse-like, smile, 'not at the extreme. I'm right at the heart, the very centre, of Christianity.'

Daniel Bartlett had something. The Anglican establishment often looks at itself and sees itself midway between Catholic and Evangelical extremes. But that depends upon one's point of viewing. Suppose you were to take the full perspective of worldwide Christianity? Suddenly it all looks different. Consider the continuum. Right in the centre stands the Anglican Evangelical. He has retained the major essentials of historic Catholic and Orthodox Christianity – creeds, episcopacy, three-fold ministry, sacramental liturgy. But there is another side to him. He, like all the Christians who look back to the Reformation with gratitude, uses his Bible as a sure guide. He knows what it is to seek for, and usually to experience, a personal conversion. He cannot rest content with the outward signs of Catholicity – he looks for a felt spiritual experience within a shared 'priesthood of all believers'. The Anglican Evangelical has, in short, discovered himself at the pivotal point of worldwide Christianity. He is the butt of those on both sides who believe he has sold out to the others. Too Catholic for the Protestants: too Protestant for the Catholics. If he has eyes to see this he does not feel ashamed. He is encouraged. He sees the virtues of a blend of continuity and spontaneity, of objectivity and subjectivity.

That, then, for those who have their eyes open, is the Anglican Evangelical's destiny. Having lost touch with it for half a century he has recently rediscovered his inheritance and it has led him to flourish for twenty-five years. But what of the future? Is the ball really at the feet of the Evangelicals and, supposing that to be the case, have enough of them noticed it and do they have sufficient interest and enthusiasm either to want to kick it or to know in which direction the goal lies?

Twice in the last few weeks I have heard that question earnestly discussed. On both occasions able representatives of the 'under forty-five' clergy have been present. They, after all, are best placed to know their own contemporaries. Out come the opinions and they are not one bit triumphalist. There aren't many up-and-coming leaders in the top flight. Many of the rank and file just want to be left to do the job in the parish. Pietism flourishes.

This is the disturbing legacy of the 1960s and 1970s. A generation brought up on guitars, choruses, and home group discussions. Educated, as one of them put it to me, not to use words with precision because the image is dominant, not the word. Equipped not to handle doctrine but rather to 'share'. A compassionate, caring generation, suspicious of definition and labels, uneasy at, and sometimes incapable of, being asked to wrestle with sustained didactic exposition of theology. Excellent when it comes to providing religious music, drama, and art. Not so good when asked to preach and teach the Faith or to express it in writing. As a publisher said to me recently, 'where is the next Michael Green?'

It will be obvious that I share Colin Buchanan's conviction that 'all is not well'. In his view, 'there is no properly tested tradition of spirituality with any vigour today' and 'there is little evidence . . . of any wide and deep doctrinal and creative understanding of the faith'. He is referring to Anglican Evangelicals specifically in so writing.[127]

Quite apart from the reasons already adduced, I believe that there is another. Most of the clergy of previous eras were likely to spend between forty and forty-five years in their ministry. If they showed evidence of real leadership they would almost certainly be catching the constituency's eye by their late twenties or early thirties. The Church at large might well know their names within a further five to seven years. Today's Anglican Evangelical leaders are mostly in their fifties and have been 'names' for twenty years or more. They were almost all ordained in their middle-twenties and many had been National Service officers while teenagers.

Today's ordinands are generally reaching the diaconate in their late twenties and early thirties. Only the most outstanding are likely to make their mark under the age of forty and with retirement at about sixty-five to sixty-seven their anticipated 'leadership span' will be much shorter and later than in the last half-century. In short, the likelihood of anyone in the Church of England approaching the episcopal 'Trans-Siberian journey' of David Say, Bishop of Rochester since 1961 (and still running), is highly improbable!

This 'short-service' concept of ministry (thirty-five years instead of forty-five) is bound to affect future leadership patterns and in a movement like that of the Evangelicals, where the temptation to parochial pietism is endemic, its lasting effect could be very damaging.

Triumphalism is, then, highly inappropriate in the late 1980s. The growing numbers of Evangelical ordinands may conceivably have no more lasting effect on Anglican leadership than they did at the same stage in the nineteenth century. Certainly they have hardly made much impact on the General Synod's House of Clergy in the last ten years.

Then there is the question of 'Top Cat'. One of the enduring marks of Evangelicalism has been its evident need for, and subservience towards, its Napoleonic leaders. Since the 1780s figures like Simeon, Wilberforce, Shaftesbury, Ryle, Taylor Smith, Stott, Packer, Schaeffer, and Watson – not all of them Anglicans – have been placed on pedestals and uncritically hero-worshipped. Many Evangelicals seem to have this inner need for a dependable Führer-figure. Not, I hasten to add, that all those named sought or wanted such treatment. Nevertheless for periods, long or short, they got it. Today no such figure holds the limelight, universally acclaimed and followed. It will be instructive to see whether the movement can hold together without its single focal figure or whether the next High-Cockalorum will emerge and, if so, who he (could it even be a she?) will be.

I have mentioned Keele and Nottingham on various occasions and spoken of their significance in the emergence of the Anglican Evangelical growth in the past two decades. If Keele changed the geography, Nottingham modified the sociology. But what of the coming NEAC 3? A huge gathering is planned for May 1988 and while the acronym is the same, one word has been altered. Keele and Nottingham were styled 'National Evangelical Anglican Congress'. NEAC 3 is to be a 'National Evangelical Anglican Celebration'. The title has caused some concern among those who fear that 'Celebration' means a massive dose of arm-waving rather than the brain-storming which characterised NEAC 1 and NEAC 2. Will NEAC 3 be no more than an emotive jamboree, proving beyond doubt that the Pietists have stormed the citadel?

Time alone will answer that question but I think it is most unlikely. Gavin Reid and I are the only two people who have served on all three NEAC committees and we both agree that while each has been distinctly different from its predecessor the common ground remains intact. Grandson-of-Keele looks as if it is going to blend worship, fellowship, and hard work in well-balanced proportions. Its themes will closely relate to those of the 1988 Lambeth Conference and, hopefully, the Lambeth Fathers will not be unaware of what is said and done.

In the meantime, we could do well to reconsider the ideals which animated Nottingham in 1977. As that Congress drew to its close it affirmed the following 'Declarations of Intent'.[128] Viewed again after a space of ten years, hardly a word is irrelevant or out of date:–

> We have met together in the name of Jesus Christ at the second National Evangelical Anglican Congress at Nottingham. We thank God for our evangelical heritage in the Church of England. Today, we reaffirm Christ's Lordship over our lives and therefore commit ourselves to the following particular Declarations of Intent.
> 1. We bind ourselves to proclaim, explore and defend against current misconceptions the biblical faith in the deity of Jesus Christ and in his role as the only Saviour of men through his death in our place and his risen life.
> 2. We acknowledge that our handling of inspired and authoritative Scripture has often been clumsy and our interpretation of it shoddy, and we resolve to seek a more-disciplined understanding of God's holy Word.
> 3. Rejoicing in the grace and gifts of God that 'charismatic'

and 'non-charismatic' evangelicals find in each other, we pledge ourselves to work with and learn from each other in mutual trust and common dependence on the Holy Spirit.

4. In grief that we find ourselves at a distance from our evangelical brothers in other denominations, we undertake to seek closer fellowship and cooperation with them in informal consultation, in shared worship and in united outreach.

5. We recognise that all members of the body of Christ depend upon each other's ministry, and we pledge ourselves to seek ways of making this fellowship more effective in all our churches.

6. We reaffirm our commitment to the goal of visible unity in Christ's Church and declare our conviction that the starting point of visible unity is a common confession of faith in Christ, leading on to the fellowship of congregations at the Lord's table.

7. Deeply regretting past attitudes of indifference and ill will towards Roman Catholics, we renew our commitment to seek with them the truth of God and the unity he wills, in obedience to our common Lord on the basis of Scripture.

8. We repent of our lack of urgency in mission and resolve with God's help to establish as the priority in all our churches the task of making Christ fully known.

9. We repent that we have been backward in facing issues of social responsibility and in accepting social and political involvement in obedience to Christ, and we acknowledge that we have a duty to take action in our local situations for the well-being of our neighbour and against all that is unjust, dehumanising, sub-Christian and dishonouring to God.

10. Because we have often been ignorant and ill-informed Christians through neglect of study, we commit ourselves to develop realistic programmes of Christian learning as a regular part of the life of all our churches.

11. We repent of the narrowness of our Christian interest and vision, and we undertake to maintain informed and active concern for the worldwide spread of the gospel, for the stewardship of the world's resources and for the cause of welfare and justice among all men.

12. We admit that we have often tolerated low standards in our

worship and apathy in our spiritual life, and we pledge ourselves by prayer and action to seek renewal in our local churches.

Pious words, perhaps. Nevertheless they do show that Anglican Evangelicals in 1977 were honest enough to admit to some of their evident failings and prepared to tell the world of their aspirations.

No, I wouldn't agree to the title 'Evangelicals on the March' for this book. We aren't a mighty army, goose-stepping to a well-drilled victory. At the moment there isn't anyone up front on the white horse, quite a few of the regiments are out of step, there are too many stragglers and even the odd deserter slips off. Happily, the band is still playing and heads are held high. We're on the move, most of us are singing 'Tipperary', and my heart's right there.

References

1. G. R. Balleine, *A History of the Evangelical Party*, 1908: 50.
2. M. Loane, *Masters of the English Reformation*, 1954: 8.
3. Loane, *ibid.*, 28.
4. T. S. Eliot, *Little Gidding*.
5. A. G. Dickens, *The English Reformation* 1964: 400.
6. Dickens, *ibid.*, 400.
7. Dickens, *ibid.*, 400.
8. N. Sykes, *The English Religious Tradition*, 1953: 18.
9. Sykes, *ibid.*, 18–19.
10. Sykes, *ibid.*, 25.
11. Sykes, *ibid.*, 25.
12. Sykes, *ibid.*, 24.
13. D. Edwards, *Christian England* Vol. 2, 1983: 97.
14. Dickens, *op. cit.*, 426.
15. Dickens, *ibid.*, 426.
16. Dickens, *ibid.*, 426.
17. Dickens, *ibid.*, 428.
18. Sykes, *op. cit.*, 25.
19. Sykes, *ibid.*, 25.
20. Edwards, *op. cit.*, 100.
21. Edwards, *ibid.*, 170.
22. Edwards, *ibid.*, 367.
23. Edwards, *ibid.*, 304.
24. Sykes, *op. cit.*, 59.
25. Sykes, *ibid.*, 63.
26. Balleine, *op. cit.* 1933 edn: 10.
27. M. Loane, *Oxford and the Evangelical Succession*, 1950: 23–24.
28. Loane, *ibid.*, 20.
29. Loane, *ibid.*, 20.
30. Loane, *ibid.*, 25.
31. Loane, *ibid.*, 27.
32. J. C. Ryle, *Christian Leaders of the Last Century*, 1880: 36.
33. Loane, *op. cit.*, 31.
34. Loane, *ibid.*, 41.
35. Loane, *ibid.*, 41.
36. S. C. Carpenter, *Church and People* Vol. 1, 1933: 28.
37. M. Loane, *Cambridge and the Evangelical Succession*, 1952: 104–105.
38. W. Lecky, *A History of England in the Eighteenth Century* Vol. 2, 1892: 627.
39. Ryle, *op. cit.*, 130.

40. M. Hennell, *John Venn and the Clapham Sect*, 1958: 14.
41. E. P. Thompson, *The Making of the English Working Class*, 1963: 430.
42. G. M. Trevelyan, *English Social History*, 1944: 493.
43. F. K. Brown, *Fathers of the Victorians*, 1961: 62.
44. D. Samuel, ed. *The Evangelical Succession*, 1979: 71.
45. H. P. Liddon, *Life of E. B. Pusey* Vol. 1, 1894: 255.
46. Sykes, *op. cit.*, 71.
47. C. Smyth, *The Church and the Nation*, 1962: 148.
48. H. G. C. Moule, *Charles Simeon*, 1948: 151.
49. Samuel, *op. cit.*, 73.
50. Samuel, *ibid.*, 73.
51. Samuel, *ibid.*, 74.
52. G. Battiscombe, *Shaftesbury*, 1974: 264.
53. D. Edwards, *Christian England* Vol. 3, 1984: 172.
54. Battiscombe, *op. cit.*, 264.
55. O. Chadwick, *The Victorian Church* Vol. 1, 1966: 469.
56. Chadwick, *ibid.*, 476.
57. O. Chadwick, *The Founding of Cuddesdon*, 1954: 4.
58. C. O. Buchanan, *article: Anvil* Vol. 1, No. 1, 1984: 7.
59. Battiscombe, *op. cit.*, 269.
60. Buchanan, *op. cit.*, 8.
61. R. Manwaring, *From Controversy to Co-existence*, 1985: 2.
62. A. P. Stanley, *Life of Dr. Arnold* Vol. 1, 1881: 246.
63. Samuel, *op. cit.*, 80–81.
64. C. S. Lewis, *Poems*, 1964: 55.
65. R. Brooke, *Oxford Dictionary of Quotations*, 1981: 94.
66. S. Sassoon, *Selected Poems*, 1968: 24.
67. S. Sassoon, *Memoirs of a Fox-hunting Man*, 1971: 247.
68. D. Johnson, *Contending for the Faith*, 1979: 92.
69. Manwaring, *op. cit.*, 34.
70. Royal Commission, *Report on Ecclesiastical Discipline*, 1906: 72.
71. Royal Commission, *ibid.*
72. W. Joynson-Hicks, *The Prayer Book Crisis*, 100, 175–178.
73. Manwaring, *op. cit.*, 54.
74. Manwaring, *ibid.*, 55.
75. Manwaring, *ibid.*, 46.
76. O. Chadwick, *Hensley Henson*, 1983: 193.
77. Balleine, *op. cit.*, 314.
78. P. Crowe, ed., *Keele '67 Report*, 1967: 7.
79. Crowe, *ibid.*, 7.
80. Crowe, *ibid.*, 15–16.
81. Crowe, *ibid.*, 15.
82. Manwaring, *op. cit.*, 177.
83. Crowe, *op. cit.*, various.
84. Crowe, *ibid.*, 16.
85. *The Independent*, 28 October 1986.

86. B. Meeking, ed., *The Evangelical-Roman Catholic Dialogue on Mission*, 1986: 16–17.
87. J. R. W. Stott, ed., *Obeying Christ in a Changing World* Vol. 1, 1977: 120–121.
88. Ordinal, *Alternative Service Book*, 1980: 387.
89. D. Skeats, ed., *Proceedings of the 1986 Anglican Evangelical Assembly*.
90. Crowe, *op. cit.*, 36.
91. G. Dix, *The Shape of the Liturgy*, 1945: 720.
92. C. O. Buchanan, *Evangelical Anglicans and Liturgy*, 1984: 5.
93. Buchanan, *ibid.*, 9.
94. Crowe, *op. cit.*, 34.
95. J. R. W. Stott, ed., *The Nottingham Statement*, 1977: 28.
96. R. Rutt, *Godparents: General Synod Miscellaneous Paper*, 202.
97. Buchanan, *op. cit.*, 12.
98. C. Porthouse, ed., *Ministry in the Seventies*, 1970: 90–102.
99. M. Saward, *All Change*, 1983: 33–60.
100. J. Edwin Orr, *Light of the Nations*, 1965: 166.
101. J. N. D. Anderson, for example: *Into the World*, 1969.
102. J. D. Douglas, ed., *Evangelicals and Unity*, 1964: 33.
103. Crowe, *op. cit.*, 36.
104. Crowe, *ibid.*, 36.
105. J. I. Packer, *The Evangelical Anglican Identity Problem*, 1978.
106. Samuel, *op. cit.*, 105.
107. M. C. Perry, ed., *Report of the Lambeth Conference*, 1978: 5.
108. D. McGavran, *Bridges of God*, 1955.
109. P. Crowe, ed., *Keele '67 Report*, 1967: 22–23.
110. Crowe, *ibid.*, 21–22.
111. Meeking, *op. cit.*, 18.
112. House of Bishops, *The Nature of Christian Belief*, 1986: 5–6.
113. House of Bishops, *ibid.*, 4.
114. Vatican 2, *Dogmatic Constitution on Divine Revelation*, 1965: 10.
115. General Synod, *Canons of the Church of England*, 1986: Canon C15.
116. Meeking, *op. cit.*, 21.
117. Meeking, *ibid.*, 20.
118. *The Independent*, 16 May 1987.
119. W. Temple, *Nature, Man, and God*, 1934: 308.
120. I. Cundy, ed., *Obeying Christ in a Changing World* Vol. 2, 1977: 114.
121. General Synod, *Report of Proceedings*, November 1986: 869, 875, 976.
122. General Synod, *ibid.*, 783.
123. E. Schillebeeckx, *Ministry*, 1980: 150, note 20.
124. P. Toon, *What's the Difference?* 1983.
125. Stott, *op. cit.*, 46–52.
126. D. J. Atkinson, *Homosexuals in the Christian Fellowship*, 1979: 95.
127. C. O. Buchanan, *article: Anvil* Vol. 1, No. 1, 1984: 15–16.
128. Stott, *op. cit.*, 76–77.